LOW CHOLESTEROL COOKBOOK
New Edition, All New Recipes

This book is for people who take an interest in their health, not just for people who need to lower their cholesterol level.
The recipes are delicious, easy to prepare, suitable for day-to-day family meals and even for special occasions.
There are over 200 recipes to inspire you, containing not only all the necessary ingredients to help lower your cholesterol count but also equally important high-fibre foods.
We firmly believe that you should still enjoy eating while tackling cholesterol. This books shows you how.
To be completely successful, don't just have an occasional low-cholesterol meal, try to re-think all your eating in line with the sorts of recipes given here.
You'll be pleasantly surprised how much fun it can be!

CONTENTS

Editor Philip Gore **Design** Craig Osment **Art Director** Stephen Joseph **Cookery Editor** Loukie Werle **Food Stylist** Wendy Berecry **Home Economist** Belinda Warn **Photography** Warren Webb **Editorial Production** Margaret Gore & Associates **Typesetting** APT Pty Ltd **Printed** in Hong Kong by Dai Nippon **Published** by Century Magazines Pty Ltd, 216-224 Commonwealth Street, Surry Hills, NSW 2010, Australia **UK Distribution** T.B. Clarke (UK) Distributors, Beckett House, 14 Billing Road, Northampton NN1 5AW. Phone: (0604) 230941; Fax (0604) 230942 **Australian Distribution** (Supermarkets) Select Magazines Pty Ltd, Suite 402, 7 Merriwa Street, Gordon, NSW 2072 (Newsagents) NDD, 150 Bourke Road, Alexandria, NSW 2015 © **Century Magazines Pty Ltd** *Recommended retail price **Photography Credits** We gratefully acknowledge **David Jones** Bondi Junction; **Barbara's House and Garden** Birkenhead Point; **Australia East India Company** Bondi Junction; **Villa Italiana** Mosman; **Accoutrement** Mosman; **Fred Pazotti** Woollahra; **Made Where** Double Bay; **The Design Store** Spit Junction; **Opus** Paddington; **Hale Imports** Brookvale; **Casa Shopping** Darlinghurst; **Country Floors** Woollahra.

What is Cholesterol?

Cholesterol is a fatty substance which is produced in our body, as well as being present in foods of animal origin like dairy products, egg yolk, meat, fish and poultry.

Of all these, egg yolks and organ meats like brains, liver and kidney are highly concentrated forms of cholesterol.

General Information

Fats and Cooking Oils
There are three different kinds of fats:
saturated
monounsaturated
polyunsaturated

SATURATED	MONOUNSATURATED	POLYUNSATURATED
butter	avocado	almonds
beef	cashews	corn oil
cheese	olives	cottonseed oil
chocolate	olive oil	fish
coconut	peanuts	hazelnuts
coconut oil	peanut oil	margarine
egg yolk	peanut butter	mayonnaise
lard		pecans
milk		safflower oil
palm oil		soybean oil
poultry		sunflower oil
vegetable shortening		

Saturated fats raise the level of cholesterol in the blood
Monounsaturated fats can help reduce cholesterol in the blood
Polyunsaturated fats are most effective in lowering cholesterol levels in the blood
Of the above fats, butter is definitely not advisable, olive oil only when flavour is important. Use safflower oil or polyunsaturated margarine whenever possible.

Fibre

Fibre plays an important role in lowering blood cholesterol levels. The added advantage of eating a high fibre diet is almost certainly a reduction in weight.

Foods high in fibre

Grains	brown rice
	bulgar
	wholemeal pasta
	wheatgerm
	unprocessed bran
	oatbran
Cereals	oatbran
	All-Bran
	Shredded Wheat
	Old-fashioned oatmeal
Fruit	orange
	grapefruit } don't remove membranes
	mandarine
	apples
	pears } don't remove skin
	peaches
	grapes
Dried Fruit	apricots
	prunes
	apples
	raisins
Vegetables	dried beans and peas
	celery
	carrots
	broccoli
	green beans
	peas
	cabbage
	asparagus
	cauliflower
	corn
Raw vegetables	celery
	carrot
	broccoli
	cucumber
	zucchini
	lettuce

SUPERB SOUPS

Here's a selection of light, delicate soups for summer and warming, hearty soups for cold winter days — all delicious and nutritious.

Curry Soup

1 tblspn olive oil

1 tblspn margarine

⅓ cup chopped celery

⅓ cup chopped, unpeeled zucchini (courgette)

⅓ cup chopped onion

1 tblspn flour

1½ tspn curry powder

3 cups degreased chicken stock

½ cup uncooked chicken breast, cut into ¼cm (1/8in) julienne

⅓ cup cooked rice

1 Granny Smith apple, unpeeled, cut into small dice

2 tspn finely chopped fresh coriander

salt

freshly ground pepper

1 Heat olive oil and margarine in a saucepan, add celery, zucchini and onion. Saute until tender, about 10 minutes.

2 Add flour and curry powder, stir well to combine, cook 1 minute.

3 Add chicken stock, bring to a boil. Add chicken. Reduce heat to a simmer, cook 15 minutes.

4 Add rice and apple, simmer a further 20 minutes. Sprinkle with coriander. Season to taste with a little salt and freshly ground pepper. Serve hot, 1 cup per person.

Serves 4

Spicy Pumpkin Soup

2 tblspn margarine

1 large onion, chopped

1½ cups chicken stock

3 cups pumpkin puree

¼ tspn nutmeg

½ cup non fat evaporated milk

1 Heat margarine in a large saucepan over medium heat, add onion and cook for 2 minutes.

2 Add the stock, pumpkin puree and nutmeg. Simmer gently until mixture boils.

3 Stir in evaporated milk and serve immediately. Garnish with fresh chopped parsley if desired.

Serves 4

Spicy Pumpkin Soup

Vichyssoise

3 cups degreased chicken stock

2 large potatoes, peeled, thickly sliced

2 leeks, sliced

¼ cup chopped spring onion (scallion)

⅔ cup low fat milk

salt

freshly ground pepper

1 Place stock in a saucepan. Add potatoes, leeks and 2 tablespoons of the spring onions. Bring to a boil, reduce heat, cook over medium low heat until vegetables are tender, about 20 minutes.

2 Puree in a food processor until smooth, add milk. Season to taste with a little salt and freshly ground pepper. Cool.

3 Pour into a soup tureen or serving dish, cover, refrigerate at least 2 hours.

4 Serve cold, garnished with a teaspoon of chopped spring onions, 1 cup per person.

Serves 4

Mushroom Soup

1 bunch spring onions (scallions)

315g (10oz) fresh mushrooms

2½ cups degreased chicken stock

1 tblspn dry sherry

1 tspn chopped fresh thyme

nutmeg, 1 twist of the mill

freshly ground black pepper

1 Cut spring onions into 5cm (2in) lengths, place in a food processor. Chop. Remove to a saucepan.

2 Wipe mushrooms with a damp cloth, place in a food processor. Chop. Combine with spring onions in the saucepan.

3 Add about 2 tablespoons of the chicken stock and the sherry, saute until vegetables are soft, about 10 minutes. Season with thyme, nutmeg and pepper.

4 Add remaining chicken stock, bring to a boil, reduce heat, simmer 30 minutes. Serve hot, ¾ cup per person.

Serves 4

Basil and Almond Soup

4 tblspn safflower oil

1 onion, chopped

2 cloves garlic, crushed

¼ cup slivered almonds

4 cups chicken stock

¼ tspn cracked black pepper

¼ cup fresh basil, chopped

1 cup broken pieces of spaghetti

1 Heat oil in a large saucepan over medium heat. Add onion, garlic and almonds, cook until onions are transparent.

2 Stir in stock, pepper and basil, cover saucepan and simmer for 10 minutes.

3 Bring a large saucepan of water to the boil, add spaghetti and cook until just tender, approximately 8 minutes. Drain pasta and add to the soup.

4 Serve immediately and top with grated low cholesterol cheese if desired.

Serves 4

Basil and Almond Soup

Scallop Soup with Vermouth and Lime

185g (6oz) scallops

1 spring onion (scallion)

1 carrot

4 cups degreased chicken stock

4 slices fresh ginger

⅓ cup dry vermouth

freshly ground pepper

1 lime, very thinly sliced

1 Place scallops in freezer for 1 hour, cut into julienne strips. Set aside. Cut spring onion and carrot into julienne strips, set aside in individual bowls.

2 In a saucepan combine stock, ginger and vermouth. Bring to a boil, reduce heat, simmer about 5 minutes. Remove ginger with a slotted spoon, discard.

3 Add carrot strips, cook 2 minutes. Add scallops, cook 30 seconds. Add spring onion, cook a further minute.

4 Remove from heat, season to taste with freshly ground pepper. Ladle into 4 heated bowls, float thin slices of lime on top. Serve 1 cup per person.

Serves 4

Italian Mussel Soup

¼ cup safflower oil

1 garlic clove, crushed

1 tblspn chopped parsley

1½ cups chopped tomatoes

2½ cups tomato puree

¼ cup dry white wine

24 uncooked mussels, washed and debearded

1 tblspn light sour cream

1 In a large saucepan heat the oil over medium heat, add garlic and saute 2 minutes. Add parsley, tomatoes, tomato puree and wine. Simmer uncovered for 15 minutes.

2 Add mussels and raise heat to high, cook until shells open. Remove mussels from soup, remove mussels from their shells and return mussel meat to soup.

3 Stir in light sour cream and serve immediately.

Serves 4

Lemon Soup

Don't panic at the whole egg in this soup. Remember it's divided by four, and with a little good management you'll keep well under your target of 2 yolks per week (this includes yolks used in baking).

4 cups degreased chicken stock

¼ cup rice

½ cup small pasta shapes

1 egg

juice of 1 lemon

1 Place chicken stock in a large saucepan, bring to a boil, add rice, reduce heat, cook until rice is tender, about 18 minutes.

2 Add pasta, cook until tender.

3 Beat egg in a small bowl, whisk in lemon juice in a steady steam. Whisk in 1 cup of the hot soup.

4 Return this mixture to the pan, stirring vigorously. Bring to a boil, remove from the heat immediately, serve at once, 1 cup per person.

Serves 4

Carrot Soup with Ginger and Lime

3 tspn margarine

¼ cup chopped onion

1 clove garlic, crushed

1½ tspn finely grated fresh ginger

2 cups sliced carrots

1½ cups degreased chicken stock

1 cup water

2 limes

1 Melt margarine in a saucepan, add onion, garlic and ginger. Saute until golden, about 5 minutes.

2 Add carrots, chicken stock and water, bring to a boil, reduce heat, simmer until carrots are tender, about 18 minutes.

3 Place soup in a processor, add juice of 2 limes. Puree. Serve hot or cold. Refrigerate for at least 2 hours to serve cold, 1 cup per person.

Serves 4

Italian Mussel Soup

Winter Soup

This high-fibre soup freezes very well, therefore it's worthwhile making in large quantities.

1 cup dried lima beans
1 tblspn safflower oil
1 leek, rinsed, sliced
1 large Spanish onion, sliced
2 large garlic cloves, finely chopped
1 large carrot, sliced
6 fresh button mushrooms, sliced
4 tomatoes, peeled, seeded, chopped
1 turnip, cut into 1cm (½in) cubes
1 parsnip, cut into 1cm (½in) cubes
1 large potato, cut into 1cm (½in) cubes
4 cups shredded cabbage
1 cup sliced celery
¾ cup chopped fresh basil
4 cups degreased chicken stock
4 cups water

1 Place lima beans in a bowl with plenty of water to cover, soak overnight. Drain, rinse under cold running water. Place in a large saucepan with plenty of water, bring to a boil, reduce heat, partially cover, simmer until beans are tender. Drain, set aside.

2 Heat oil in a very large saucepan. Add leek, onion and garlic, saute until golden, about 5 minutes.

3 Add carrot, mushrooms, tomato, turnip, parsnip, potato, cabbage, celery and basil. Saute 5 minutes over moderate heat, stirring constantly. If mixture is too dry, add a little degreased stock or water.

4 Add stock and water, bring to a boil, reduce heat to medium low, cook until all vegetables are tender, about 30 minutes.

5 Add cooked lima beans, continue cooking a further 5 minutes. Season to taste with a little salt if desired, and freshly ground black pepper. Serve hot, 1 cup per person.

Serves 12

Classic Bouillabaisse

2 lobsters and tails
¼ cup olive oil
1 large onion, chopped
2 cloves garlic, crushed
2 cups tinned peeled tomatoes and juice
1 tspn dried thyme
1 tspn cracked black pepper
4 cups chicken stock
¼ cup dry white wine
2 white fish fillets, 125g (4oz) each, cut into pieces
8 green prawns (shrimp), deveined and shelled, tails intact
8 mussels, washed and debearded
basil for garnish

1 Cup up lobster meat, return flesh to the shell.

2 Heat the oil in a large saucepan over low heat. Add the onion and garlic and saute for 3 minutes.

3 Add the tomatoes and their juice, thyme, black pepper, stock and wine. Simmer for 5 minutes. Add fish pieces and simmer for a further 3 minutes.

4 Add the prawns, mussels and lobster and simmer until mussel shells open, about 5 minutes.

5 Serve soup piping hot and garnish with fresh basil.

Serves 8

Classic Bouillabaisse

Fresh Apricot Soup

Apricots have a very high pectin content, which can help reduce blood cholesterol.

1kg (2lb) fresh apricots, peeled, stoned, roughly chopped

3 tspn cornflour

¾ cup freshly squeezed orange juice

¾ cup dry white wine

¾ cup non-fat yoghurt

fresh coriander sprigs to garnish

1 Place chopped apricot in a food processor, puree, stopping at least once to scrape down the sides.

2 Combine cornflour with ¼ cup of the orange juice. Stir into the remaining orange juice and white wine in a large saucepan. Add the pureed apricots.

3 Bring to a boil over medium heat, stirring constantly. As soon as mixture comes to a boil, remove from heat. Cool.

4 Stir in yoghurt, place in a serving dish or tureen, cover, refrigerate at least 2 hours. Serve cold, ¾ cups per person, garnished with coriander sprigs.

Serves 4

> *What is cholesterol? Cholesterol is a substance manufactured by the body and found in foods derived from animal sources, but not from food derived from plant sources. We all have cholesterol. It is only when the levels become too high that it can lead to problems. Your doctor can check your blood cholesterol level.*

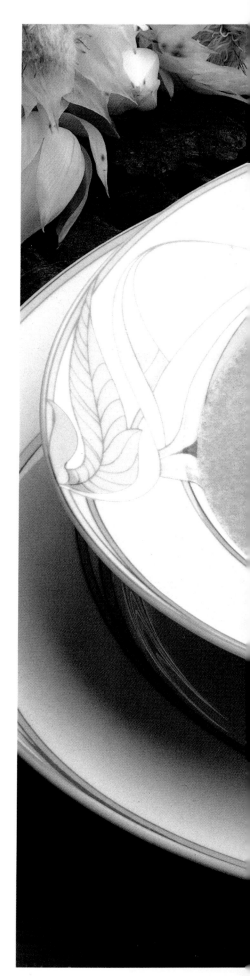

Red Lentil Soup

220g (7oz) red lentils

1 tblspn olive oil

2 carrots, finely chopped

2 onions, finely chopped

4 cups degreased chicken stock

1 tspn curry powder

1 tspn cumin

¼ tspn chilli powder

2cm (¾in) piece ginger, grated

1 Soak lentils in water overnight, drain.

2 Heat oil in large saucepan, cook onions and carrots for 5 minutes stirring occasionally. Add spices, cook 1 minute.

3 Add lentils and stock. Bring to boil, simmer, covered, for 30 minutes.

4 Blend or process in batches until smooth. Reheat without boiling.

Serves 4

Spinach Soup

1 tblspn safflower oil

1 onion, chopped

1 clove garlic, crushed

1 bunch spinach, chopped

½ cup unsweetened apple juice

½ cup freshly squeezed orange juice

1 cup degreased chicken stock

1 tspn grated fresh ginger

½ cup low fat plain yoghurt

1 Heat oil in large saucepan, cook onion and garlic 5 minutes, add spinach, apple juice, orange juice, stock and ginger. Bring to boil, reduce heat, simmer, covered 20 minutes.

2 Blend or process soup in several batches until smooth. Stir in yoghurt. Just before serving reheat soup without boiling.

Serves 4

Spinach Soup

Minestrone Soup

1 tblspn olive oil

1 onion, chopped

1 clove garlic, crushed

1 carrot, chopped

2 zucchini (courgette), chopped

1 stick celery, chopped

2 potatoes, chopped

200g (6½oz) can cannellini beans or red kidney beans, drained and rinsed

400g (13oz) can peeled tomatoes, undrained

½ tspn dried oregano

½ tspn dried basil

¼ cup tomato paste

4 cups water or degreased stock

2 cups shredded cabbage

1 cup wholewheat macaroni

2 tblspn chopped parsley

1 Heat oil in large saucepan, cook onion and garlic for 5 minutes, stirring occasionally.

2 Add carrot, zucchini, celery and potatoes, cook for 5 minutes, stirring occasionally.

3 Add beans, tomatoes, oregano, basil, tomato paste and water. Bring to boil, reduce heat, simmer, covered 30 minutes.

4 Add cabbage and macaroni, cook further 10 minutes or until macaroni is tender. Add parsley and serve.

Serves 4

Cucumber and Dill Soup

1 cucumber, peeled and chopped

3 cups degreased chicken stock

1 clove garlic, crushed

500g (16oz) carton low fat plain yoghurt

1½ tblspns lemon juice

1 tblspn chopped dill

1 Place cucumber and stock in large saucepan and bring to boil. Simmer covered for 15 minutes. Refrigerate until cold.

2 Combine garlic, yoghurt, lemon juice and dill. Stir into the chilled soup.

Serves 4

Fennel Soup

1 tblspn olive oil

1 onion, sliced

1 clove garlic, crushed

4 fennel bulbs

400g (13oz) can peeled tomatoes, undrained

½ cup tomato paste

4 cups degreased chicken stock

TOASTED ITALIAN BREAD:

1 long loaf crusty Italian bread

1 Heat oil in large saucepan, add onion and garlic, cook 5 minutes, stirring occasionally.

2 Trim and halve fennel bulbs, reserve feathery ends for garnish. Cut fennel into thin slices. Add to pan with tomatoes and tomato paste, cook 5 minutes.

3 Add stock, bring to boil, reduce heat, simmer, covered 30 minutes. Garnish with reserved feathery ends. Serve with toasted Italian bread.

4 To make toasted Italian bread: Cut bread into 2cm (¾in) slices. Bake on oven tray in moderate oven 10 minutes, turn bread, bake further 10 minutes or until golden.

Serves 4

Miso Soup

1 tblspn olive oil

1 onion, chopped

1 clove garlic, crushed

1 stick celery, chopped

1 carrot, chopped

1 parsnip, chopped

1 kumera (orange sweet potato), chopped

¼ small butternut pumpkin, chopped

1 piece corn on the cob, kernels removed

2 cups water

2 tblspn natto miso (see note)

1 Heat oil in large saucepan, cook onion and garlic for 5 minutes, stirring occasionally.

2 Add celery, carrot, parsnip, kumera, pumpkin and corn. Cook for further 5 minutes, stirring occasionally.

3 Add water, bring to boil, reduce heat, simmer, covered 30 minutes.

4 Place 2 teaspoons natto miso into each soup bowl. Ladle hot soup into bowls, serve immediately.

Serves 4

Note: Natto Miso is available from healthfood shops, especially those specialising in macrobiotic foods.

Fennel Soup

Gazpacho

400g (13oz) can peeled tomatoes, undrained

2 cloves garlic, crushed

2 tblspn wholegrain breadcrumbs (1 slice bread, crusts removed)

¼ cup tomato paste

2 tblspn lemon juice

pinch cayenne pepper

¼ tspn paprika

¼ tspn ground cumin

1 red capsicum (pepper), finely chopped

1 green capsicum (pepper), finely chopped

1 red onion, finely chopped

1 cucumber, peeled, finely chopped

1 tblspn chopped mint

2 cups iced water

1 Place tomatoes in processor with garlic, breadcrumbs, tomato paste, lemon juice, cayenne pepper, paprika and cumin. Process until smooth. Place into large bowl.

2 Add red and green capsicum, onion, cucumber and mint. Stir in iced water. Refrigerate for 1 to 2 hours.

Serves 4

Red Capsicum (Pepper) Soup

3 red capsicum (peppers)

1 tblspn olive oil

1 onion, chopped

1 clove garlic, crushed

400g (13oz) can peeled tomatoes, undrained

¼ cup tomato paste

1 cup degreased beef stock

250g (½lb) silken tofu, chopped

1 Cut capsicum in half, remove seeds. Place under hot grill, skin side up for 5 minutes or until charred. Cool slightly, chop roughly.

2 Heat oil in large saucepan, cook onion and garlic for 5 minutes. Stir occasionally. Add capsicum, tomatoes, tomato paste and stock. Bring to boil, reduce heat, simmer, covered 30 minutes. Remove from heat.

3 Add tofu. Blend or process soup in several batches until smooth. Just before serving, reheat soup without boiling.

Serves 4

Beetroot Soup

1 tblspn olive oil

1 onion, chopped

1 potato, chopped

1 carrot, chopped

2 large beetroot, washed and trimmed

6 cups degreased beef stock

2 tblspn lemon juice

½ cup low fat plain yoghurt

1 Heat oil in large saucepan, cook onion, potato and carrot 5 minutes, stirring occasionally. Add whole beetroot and stock to pan, bring to boil, reduce heat, simmer, covered 30 minutes.

2 Remove beetroot with slotted spoon. Peel and cool beetroot, chop roughly. Return to pan, bring to boil, reduce heat, simmer covered another 30 minutes.

3 Blend or process soup in several batches until smooth, strain, then add lemon juice. Serve topped with yoghurt.

Serves 4

Beetroot Soup

French Onion Soup

| 2 tblspn olive oil |
| 500g (1lb) onions, thinly sliced |
| ¼ tspn sugar |
| 2 tblspn plain flour |
| 4 cups degreased beef stock |
| ½ cup dry white wine |
| 2 tblspn brandy |
| 1 tblspn grated Parmesan cheese |

TOASTED FRENCH BREAD:

| 1 stick wholemeal French bread |
| 1 tblspn olive oil |
| 1 clove garlic |

1 Heat oil in large saucepan, cook onions over medium heat for 20 minutes, stirring occasionally. Add sugar, cook for a further 10 minutes or until golden brown.

2 Add flour, cook, stirring for 2 minutes. Remove from heat, stir in stock and wine. Bring to boil, simmer, covered for 30 minutes. Stir in brandy, simmer for 5 minutes.

3 Place rounds of bread into soup bowls, pour over hot soup, sprinkle with Parmesan cheese.

4 To make toasted French bread: Cut bread into 2cm (¾in) rounds. Rub both sides of bread with cut clove garlic, brush with oil. Place on oven tray. Bake in moderate oven 10 minutes, turn, bake further 10 minutes or until lightly browned.

Serves 4

FISH AND SEAFOOD

Fish is a source of protein, minerals and vitamins and including more fish in our diet is an excellent way of cutting down cholesterol.

Seafood Brochettes with Dill Butter Sauce

16 scallops, deveined

16 green king prawns (shrimp), deveined, shelled, tail left intact

8 button mushrooms

8 cherry tomatoes

1 capsicum (pepper), seeded, cut into 2cm (¾in) squares

⅔ cup margarine

juice of 1 lemon

¼ cup dry white wine

2 tblspn chopped fresh dill

1 Alternate 2 scallops and 2 prawns with a tomato, mushroom and piece of capsicum, on 8 soaked wooden skewers.

2 Grill under medium heat, approximately 1 minute each side, or until seafood is cooked.

3 Melt the margarine in a medium saucepan over medium heat. Add the lemon juice and wine and simmer until reduced by one third.

4 Stir in chopped dill and spoon sauce over brochettes.

Serves 4

John Dory with White Wine Pecan Sauce

1 tspn safflower oil

4 John Dory fillets, 125g (4oz) each

½ cup dry white wine

½ cup degreased chicken stock

dash of Tabasco sauce

2 tblspn chopped parsley

SAUCE:

2 tblspn safflower oil

2 tblspn plain flour

¼ cup skim milk

¼ cup degreased chicken stock

½ cup dry white wine

½ cup chopped pecan nuts

1 Brush inside of a baking dish, large enough to hold fillets in one layer, with oil. Place fillets in dish, add wine, stock and Tabasco. Cover with foil, bake in a 160°C (325°F) oven for 20 minutes, or until fish flakes easily.

2 Meanwhile make sauce: Heat oil in a saucepan over low heat. Stir in flour, cook 2 minutes, stirring constantly. Add a little salt and freshly ground pepper to taste. Add milk, stock and wine, cook over medium heat, stirring constantly, until mixture thickens. Add pecans, simmer a further minute.

3 Place cooked fillets on a heated platter, pour over sauce, serve immediately, garnished with parsley.

Serves 4

Seafood Brochettes with Dill Butter Sauce

Prawn (Shrimp) Curry

2 tblspn margarine

1 Granny Smith apple, unpeeled, cored, chopped

1 onion, chopped

1 tblspn curry powder

¼ cup plain flour

¼ tspn ground cardamom

salt

pepper

300ml (½ pint) degreased chicken stock

1 tblspn freshly squeezed lemon juice

625g (1¼lb) uncooked prawns (shrimp), shelled, deveined

Basmati rice, cooked (see note)

1 Melt margarine in a saucepan, add apple, onion and curry powder. Saute until onion is golden, about 5 minutes.

2 Off the heat stir in flour and cardamom. Add chicken stock and lemon juice, combine well.

3 Bring to a boil, reduce heat to a simmer, cook 5 minutes or until sauce thickens, stirring from time to time. Season to taste with a little salt and freshly ground black pepper.

4 Add prawns to sauce, cook until prawns change colour, stirring constantly, about 10 minutes. Serve immediately with Basmati rice.

Note: Basmati rice has a distinctly nutty flavour. It is available in Oriental food stores and most supermarkets.

Serves 6

FISH ALTERNATIVES

If some of the types of fish included in this book are unavailable, here are some suggestions for alternatives that will produce delicious results.

Snapper	—	Sea Perch
	—	Sea Bream
Ocean Perch	—	Sea Bass
	—	Turbot
Gemfish	—	Sea Bream
Ling	—	Pike
	—	Perch
Atlantic Salmon	—	Salmon
Orange Roughy	—	Sea Perch
Ocean Trout	—	Salmon Trout

Tuna Steaks with Yoghurt Cucumber Sauce

½ cup plain non fat yoghurt

3 tblspn low-joule mayonnaise

1 tblspn freshly squeezed lime juice

¼ cup grated cucumber

1 cup green seedless grapes

4 tuna steaks, 185g (6oz) each

2 tblspn margarine, melted

¼ cup lemon juice

1 In a small bowl, combine yoghurt, mayonnaise, lime juice, cucumber and grapes, set aside.

2 Brush tuna steaks with combined melted butter and lemon juice and grill under medium heat until cooked through, approximately 4 minutes each side.

3 Serve tuna with yoghurt cucumber sauce.

Serves 4

Baked Herbed Snapper

¼ cup safflower oil

1½ cups chopped onion

2 cloves garlic, crushed

425g (13½oz) can tomatoes, drained

¼ cup chopped fresh chives

¼ cup chopped fresh parsley

¼ cup chopped fresh dill

pepper

1.5kg (3lb) whole snapper, cleaned

¼ cup freshly squeezed lemon juice

1 cup julienned spring onions (scallions)

½ cup dry white wine

1 Heat oil in frying pan, add onion, saute until golden. Add garlic, tomatoes, chives, parsley and dill. Season to taste with freshly ground black pepper. Cook over moderate heat for 10 minutes, breaking up tomatoes.

2 Grind black pepper over fish, sprinkle with lemon juice. Make 3 diagonal slashes in top of fish with a sharp knife.

3 Spread tomato mixture into a baking dish large enough to hold fish, place fish on top. Cover with spring onions. Pour wine over, cover with foil.

4 Bake in a 180°C (350°F) oven for 20 minutes. Remove foil, cook a further 10 minutes or until fish flakes easily. Serve hot.

Serves 4

Snapper and Potato Casserole

1 tspn safflower oil

2 large potatoes, very thinly sliced

salt

½ onion, thinly sliced

4 tomatoes, peeled, seeded, chopped

500g (1lb) zucchini (courgette), thinly sliced

250g (½lb) button mushrooms, sliced

6 snapper fillets, 125g (4oz) each

2 tblspn freshly squeezed lemon juice

2 tblspn chopped fresh basil

4 spring onions (scallions), sliced

2 tblspn dry white wine

lemon wedges for garnish

1 Brush inside of an 8-cup baking dish with oil. Make a layer of potato slices, season with a little salt. Top with onion, cover with foil. Bake in a 180°C (350°F) oven for 15 minutes.

2 Arrange tomatoes, zucchini and mushrooms over potatoes and onions. Place fish on top, sprinkle with lemon juice, basil, spring onions and white wine.

3 Bake about 20 minutes without cover or until fish flakes easily when tested. Serve hot, garnished with lemon wedges.

Serves 6

Tuna Steaks with Yoghurt Cucumber Sauce

Ocean Perch Casserole

1½ cup chopped onion

1 cup chopped green capsicum (pepper)

¾ cup chopped celery

2 tblspn dry white wine

425g (13½oz) can tomatoes, undrained

2 tblspn chopped continental parsley

⅓ cup tomato puree

1 bay leaf

½ tspn mild curry powder

655g (1lb 5oz) ocean perch fillets, cut into 2.5cm (1in) pieces

1 Combine onion, capsicum and celery in a saucepan. Add white wine, bring to a boil. Saute until vegetables are tender, about 10 minutes.

2 Add tomatoes, parsley, tomato puree, bay leaf and curry powder. Simmer about 50 minutes, breaking up tomatoes with a wooden spoon, stirring from time to time.

3 Add fish pieces to sauce, simmer about 15 minutes, or unitl fish is cooked through.

4 Spoon into a heated serving dish, serve hot, 1 cup per person.

Serves 6

Grilled Tuna with Pink Peppercorns

4 tuna steaks, 155g (5oz) each

pepper

1 tblspn safflower oil

2 tblspn chopped continental parsley

SAUCE:

½ cup dry white wine

juice of 1 lemon

1 tblspn finely chopped onion

1 tblspn margarine

1 tblspn pink peppercorns

1 Season tuna steaks with freshly ground black papper. Brush with oil, grill until done to your liking (see note), turning once.

2 To make sauce: Combine wine, lemon juice and onion in a saucepan, bring to a boil. Continue boiling until reduced by half. Whisk in margarine and peppercorns.

3 Pour sauce over fish, sprinkle with parsley. Serve immediately.

Note: Tuna steaks do not have to be cooked to the same degree of doneness as most other fish. Some people prefer tuna just cooked on the outside, virtually raw inside.

Serves 4

Fish Parcels with Mushroom Sauce

4 gemfish fillets, 125g (4oz) each

2 tblspn lemon juice

12 sheets filo pastry

¼ cup melted margarine

1½ tblspn cornflour

½ cup cold degreased chicken stock

¾ cup skim milk

1½ cups button mushrooms, sliced

pinch nutmeg

1 Lightly season fish with salt and pepper, brush with lemon juice.

2 Divide filo into four piles, 3 sheets in each. Brush margarine between each sheet.

3 Place fish fillet on each pile of filo and roll each one up into a parcel, tucking in ends.

4 Place fish parcels seamside down on a greased baking tray. Bake in a moderate oven for 20 minutes.

5 To make sauce: Combine cornflour with chicken stock to make a thin paste. Add the milk and pour into a small saucepan. Heat gently, stirring constantly, until sauce begins to thicken, add mushrooms and nutmeg, cook a further 3 minutes. Serve sauce over parcels.

Serves 4

Fish Parcels with Mushroom Sauce

Ling Fillets with Asparagus Souffle

4 ling fillets, 185g (6oz) each
1 tblspn lemon juice
2 tblspn margarine
pepper
12 stalks asparagus, steamed
⅔ cup low fat yoghurt
2 tblspn horseradish
2 tblspn finely chopped spring onions (scallions)
1 egg white
2 tblspn chopped continental parsley

1 Sprinkle ling fillets with lemon juice, brush with margarine, season to taste with freshly ground pepper. Place under a heated grill, cook about 8 minutes, turning once, or until fish is very nearly done.

2 Cut asparagus stalks to same length as fillets; place 3 stalks on each fillet.

3 In a small bowl combine yoghurt with horseradish and spring onions.

4 In another bowl beat egg white until stiff peaks form. Combine with yoghurt mixture, spread onto fillets and asparagus to cover.

5 Return to grill, cook until golden and puffed. Serve immediately, garnish with parsley.

Serves 4

Marinated Atlantic Salmon

4 Atlantic salmon cutlets, 185g (6oz) each
MARINADE:
⅓ cup lemon juice
¼ cup dry vermouth
1 tblspn olive oil
2 tblspn tomato ketchup
2 cloves garlic, bruised
1 tspn marjoram
¼ cup chopped parsley
salt

Octopus Cocktail

1 Place salmon cutlets in a dish large enough to hold fish in one layer.

2 To make marinade: Combine all ingredients in a screwtop jar, season to taste with salt, shake until well blended.

3 Pour marinade over salmon, cover, refrigerate for at least 24 hours.

4 Remove salmon with slotted spoon, reserve marinade. Brush griller tray with a little oil, cook salmon until flesh flakes easily, about 10 minutes, turning once. Place on a heated platter.

5 Meanwhile heat marinade in a little saucepan, pour over cooked salmon cutlets, serve immediately.

Serves 4

Octopus Cocktail

2 cups tenderised baby octopus, heads and beaks removed
½ cup lemon juice
2 tspn sambal oelek, or chilli paste
½ cup tomato sauce
¼ cup low-joule coleslaw dressing
¼ tspn Tabasco sauce

1 Wash and drain octopus tentacles. Bring a large saucepan with 2 cups of water to the boil, add lemon juice, sambal oelek and octopus.

2 Boil octopus for approximately 1 minute or until just cooked through. Drain and chill.

3 To serve, arrange a few lettuce leaves in 4 serving glasses and arrange octopus on top.

4 Combine tomato sauce, coleslaw dressing and Tabasco sauce, pour dressing over octopus.

Serves 4

Crispy Baked Gemfish Pieces

Crispy Baked Gemfish Pieces

750g (1½lb) gemfish fillets, cut into 3cm (1¼in) square pieces

freshly ground black pepper

3 tblspn safflower oil

½ cup cornflake crumbs

1 lemon, cut into quarters

1 Wash and pat fish dry with paper towels. Season with black pepper and toss in oil. Lightly coat each fish piece with cornflake crumbs.

2 Arrange fish in a single layer in a lightly oiled baking dish. Bake in a moderately hot oven for 10 minutes.

3 Sprinkle lemon juice over fish pieces just before serving and garnish with fresh lemon and parsley.

Serves 6

Grilled Chilli Fillets

4 orange roughy fillets, 125g (4oz) each

1 tblspn Worcestershire sauce

1 tblspn safflower oil

1 tspn soy sauce

¼ tspn chilli powder

1 clove garlic, crushed

few drops Tabasco sauce

1 Place fillets in a baking dish large enough to hold fish in one layer.

2 Combine remaining ingredients in a screwtop jar, shake until well blended. Pour over fish fillets.

3 Place baking dish under a heated grill, cook about 8 minutes without turning, or until fish flakes easily. Serve immediately.

Serves 4

Lemon and Coriander Ocean Trout

4 ocean trout fillets, 185g (6oz) each

½ tspn mild paprika

½ cup chopped fresh coriander

juice of ½ lemon

2 tblspn dry white wine

2 tblspn margarine, melted

coriander sprigs for garnish

1 Place fillets in a shallow baking dish. Sprinkle with paprika and coriander, pour over lemon juice and wine, then margarine.

2 Place dish under a heated grill, cook until fish flakes easily, about 10 minutes. Garnish with coriander sprigs. Serve hot.

Serves 4

Fish are rich in polyunsaturated fat, however most fish contain less fat than meat. You can eat any fish, with the exception of prawns (shrimp), lobster, oysters, mussels and crayfish: which are allowed only in moderation.

Barbecued Kebabs

500g (1lb) ling fillets, cubed

1 cup unsweetened apple cider

1 tspn dried tarragon

1 tblspn chopped fresh mint

1 tblspn chopped fresh chives

½ pineapple, peeled and cubed

½ rockmelon, peeled and cubed

2 apples, cubed, soaked in lemon juice

4 Lebanese cucumbers, cubed

12 bamboo skewers, soaked in water

1 Cut fish into 2.5cm (1in) cubes. Marinate fish in combined cider, tarragon, mint and chives in dish for 20 minutes.

2 Cut pineapple, rockmelon, apples and cucumbers into 2.5cm (1in) cubes.

3 Thread fish onto skewers alternately with fruit and cucumber.

4 Barbecue or grill about 7 minutes, turning once. Baste with marinade during cooking.

Makes 12

Baked Fish and Vegetables

4 mullet fillets

1 stick celery, sliced

4 spring onions (scallion), chopped

1 small red capsicum (pepper), chopped

400g (13oz) can tomatoes, chopped, undrained

2 tblspn dry white wine

1 tspn dried basil

1 Arrange fillets in single layer in lightly oiled shallow ovenproof dish.

2 Sprinkle vegetables, wine and basil on top. Cover with foil.

3 Bake in moderate oven 20 minutes or until just cooked.

Serves 4

Barbecued Kebabs

Grilled Mustard Cutlets

4 fish cutlets, 185g (6oz) each

1 tblspn grainy mustard

1 tspn honey

2 tblspn dry white wine

1 clove garlic, crushed

1 Combine mustard, honey, wine and garlic.

2 Dip cutlets into mixture, coat on both sides. Stand 30 minutes.

3 Line griller with a piece of lightly oiled foil. Grill cutlets until golden on both sides and just cooked. Turn only once during cooking.

Serves 4

Orange Fish Parcels

2 tspn olive oil

4 white fish fillets, 185g (6oz) each skin and bones removed

1 tspn grated orange rind

¼ cup freshly squeezed orange juice

1 tspn chopped fresh dill

1 tblspn chopped fresh chives

½ tspn soy sauce

1 Cut out 4 x 30cm (12in) square pieces foil, brush with oil.

2 Place one fish fillet in centre of each square.

3 Combine orange rind, orange juice, dill, chives and soy sauce. Sprinkle mixture over fillets.

4 Wrap up and bake parcels on ovent tray in moderate oven 15 minutes. Serve in foil.

Serves 4

Greek Snapper in Oven Bag

4 snapper fillets, 155g (5oz) each

1 tblspn olive oil

1 onion, sliced

1 stick celery, sliced

1 green capsicum (pepper), sliced

1 tomato, sliced

1 lemon, sliced

¼ cup dry white wine

1 tspn dried oregano leaves

1 Heat oil in pan, cook onion, celery and green capsicum for 5 minutes. Arrange fish in single layer in oven bag.

2 Top with cooked onion mixture. Arrange sliced tomato and lemon on top. Sprinkle with wine and oregano. Seal bag.

3 Bake in moderate oven 30 minutes or until fish flakes easily with a fork.

Serves 4

Steamed Snapper with Tamari and Ginger

4 snapper or ocean trout fillets, 185g (6oz) each

2 tblspn tamari or shoyu (see note)

1 tspn sesame oil

1 tspn grated green ginger

1 tblspn lemon juice

1 Remove skin and excess bones from fillets. Arrange in a single layer in steamer (or in shallow dish to microwave).

Greek Snapper in Ovenbag.

2 Combine tamari, sesame oil, ginger and lemon juice. Brush mixture over fish.

3 Cover and steam 5 minutes (or microwave on High 5 minutes) or until just cooked.

Serves 4

Note: Tamari or shoyu are available from healthfood shops.

Sweet and Sour Whiting

500g (1lb) whiting fillets, skin and bones removed
2 tspn olive oil
1 onion, cut into petals
1 clove garlic, crushed
1 red capsicum (pepper), cut into diamonds
1 green capsicum (pepper), cut into diamonds
1 stick celery, sliced
400g (13oz) can unsweetened pineapple pieces, undrained
1 tblspn cornflour
1 tblspn vinegar
1 tblspn soy sauce
¼ cup water

1 Cut whiting into bite-sized pieces.

2 Heat oil in pan, stir-fry onion 5 minutes. Add garlic, capsicum and celery, cook 3 minutes.

3 Add pineapple with combined cornflour and vinegar, soy sauce and water. Cook stirring until mixture boils and thickens.

4 Add fish, reduce heat, simmer 5 minutes or until fish is just cooked. Serve with rice.

Serves 4

Lime and Basil Grilled John Dory

500g (1lb) John or Silver Dory fillets

½ cup lime juice

½ cup lemon juice

1 tblspn chopped fresh basil

1 tblspn chopped fresh chives

ground black pepper

1 Marinate fish in remaining ingredients in a dish for 30 minutes.

2 Line grill with lightly oiled foil, place fillets skin side down, cook under hot grill 6 minutes, do not turn. Baste with marinade during cooking.

Serves 4

Curried Seafood

410g (13oz) ling fillets

125g (4oz) mussel meat

125g (4oz) scallops

1 tblspn olive oil

1 onion, sliced

2 tspn curry powder

1 tspn ground cumin

½ tspn ground turmeric

½ tspn ground ginger

1 cup water

1 tblspn cornflour

1 tblspn water, extra

½ cup low fat plain yoghurt

1 Cut ling into bite-sized pieces.

2 Heat oil in pan, cook onion 5 minutes. Add curry powder, cumin, turmeric and ginger, cook stirring 1 minute.

3 Add water, bring to boil, add ling. Reduce heat, simmer 5 minutes.

4 Add combined cornflour and extra water, cook until mixture boils and thickens.

5 Add mussels and scallops, cook 1 minute.

6 Add yoghurt, heat but do not boil. Serve with Basmati rice (see note).

Serves 4

Note: Basmati rice is available from supermarkets and specialty food shops.

Fish au Gratin

4 ling fillets, 185g (6oz) each

2 tblspn lemon juice

1 tblspn chopped parsley

4 spring onion (scallins), chopped

½ tspn dried dill

1 tblspn olive oil

½ cup fresh breadcrumbs

1 Arrange fillets in lightly oiled shallow ovenproof dish. Sprinkle lemon juice, parsley, spring onions and dill over fish.

2 Heat oil in pan, add breadcrumbs, cook stirring until golden brown. Spread browned breadcrumbs over fish.

3 Bake in moderate oven 15 minutes or until fish is just cooked. Serve with salad.

Serves 4

Lime and Basil Grilled John Dory

Hot, Meatless, Main Dishes

You don't have to be a firm vegetarian to enjoy these delicious dishes. They are ideal for those meat-free days we should all include in our weekly menus.

Spinach Souffle

200g (6½oz) English spinach, finely chopped

30g (1oz) polyunsaturated margarine

2 tblspn plain wholemeal flour

¾ cup skim milk

2 tblspn grated Gruyere or Edam cheese

¼ tspn paprika

4 egg whites

1 Cook spinach in steamer until wilted. Press against sieve to remove excess water.

2 Melt margarine in pan, add flour, cook 1 minute. Gradually add milk, cook, stirring until sauce boils and thickens.

3 Stir in cheese, paprika and spinach.

4 Oil a souffle dish. Beat egg whites until firm peaks form. Fold egg whites into spinach mixture.

5 Pour mixture into souffle dish, bake in moderately hot oven 35 minutes. Serve immediately.

Serves 4

Stuffed Golden Nugget Pumpkins

4 golden nugget pumpkins

¼ cup oil

FILLING:

2 tspn olive oil

1 onion, chopped

½ tspn chilli powder

2 tblspn ground cumin

1 clove garlic, crushed

¼ cup tomato paste

¼ cup dry white wine

400g (13oz) can tomatoes, undrained

400g (13oz) can red kidney beans, drained

1 Cut a 3cm (1¼in) lid from each pumpkin, scoop out seeds, Brush inside of each pumpkin with oil, place pumpkins on oven tray, place oiled lids on top; bake in moderate oven 30 minutes.

2 To make filling: Heat oil in large pan, cook onion 5 minutes, add chilli, cumin and garlic, cook 1 minute.

3 Add tomato paste, wine, tomatoes and beans. Cook over low heat, stirring occasionally for about 20 minutes or until mixture is thick.

Serves 4

Stuffed Golden Nugget Pumpkins

Vegetarian Potato Pie

3 medium potatoes, peeled

2 small carrots, peeled

1 small onion, peeled

1 clove garlic, crushed

2 egg whites

1 tblspn olive oil

2 tblspn chopped parsley

2 tblspn wholemeal breadcrumbs

½ cup skim milk powder

15g (½oz) polyunsaturated margarine

½ cup grated Edam cheese

½ cup low fat plain yoghurt

2 spring onions (scallions), chopped

1 Grate potatoes, carrots and onion in bowl, add garlic. Add lightly beaten egg whites, oil, parsley, breadcrumbs and milk powder.

2 Spread into well greased 20cm (8in) pie dish, dot with margarine, bake in moderate oven 30 minutes, sprinkle with cheese, bake further 15 minutes. Serve hot or cold topped with combined yoghurt and spring onions.

Serves 4

Asparagus Quiche with filo Pastry

6 sheets filo pastry

1 tblspn olive oil

340g (11oz) can asparagus, drained

4 spring onions (scallions), chopped

1 tspn olive oil, extra

4 egg whites, beaten

½ cup skim milk

1 tblspn plain flour

250g (½lb) low fat cottage cheese

1 tblspn lemon juice

250g can tuna in brine, drained

1 tblspn chopped parsley

1 tspn paprika

1 Line lightly oiled 20cm (8in) quiche dish (not with removable base) with one sheet filo pastry. Lightly brush with oil, layer remaining sheets, brush between layers with oil. Use scissors to trim pastry.

2 Heat extra oil in small pan, add spring onions, cook 3 minutes, cool. Combine spring onions in bowl with egg whites, skim milk, flour, cottage cheese, lemon juice, tuna and parsley. Spread over pastry.

3 Arrange asparagus spears on top. Sprinkle with paprika. Bake in moderate oven 40 minutes.

Serves 4

Vegetable Strudel

3 cups broccoli flowerets

3 cups cauliflower flowerets

1 tspn olive oil

1 onion, finely chopped

1 tblspn cornflour

1 cup skim milk

pinch nutmeg

2 tblspn grated Parmesan cheese

60g (2oz) grated mozzarella cheese

8 sheets filo pastry

2 tblspns olive oil, extra

1 Cook broccoli and cauliflower in steamer or microwave until just tender, drain.

2 Heat oil in pan, cook onion 5 minutes. Add combined cornflour, milk and nutmeg. Cook until sauce boils and thickens. Remove from heat, stir in Parmesan cheese.

3 Add cooked broccoli and cauliflower, mix well.

4 Place a sheet of filo pastry on bench, brush lightly with extra oil, repeat layering with remaining pastry, brushing every sheet with oil.

5 Place filling along one edge of long side, leaving a 5cm (2in) border on sides and front. Fold sides in and roll up. Brush with oil. Place onto oiled oven tray. Bake in moderately hot oven 30 minutes. Serve cut into thick slices.

Serves 4

Soyaroni with Mushrooms

250g (½lb) soyaroni noodles

30g (1oz) polyunsaturated margarine

1½ tblspn plain flour

1 tspn French mustard

2½ cups skim milk

½ cup dry white wine

1 tblspn olive oil

1 onion, chopped

1 clove garlic, crushed

250g (½lb) mushrooms, sliced

2 tblspn chopped parsley

1 cup wholemeal breadcrumbs

1 tblspn grated Parmesan cheese

1 Cook soyaroni in boiling water 8 minutes or until tender, drain and rinse under hot water.

2 Meanwhile, melt margarine in saucepan, add flour and mustard, cook, stirring 1 minute. Gradually add milk and wine, cook stirring until sauce boils and thickens.

3 Heat oil in pan, cook onion 5 minutes, stirring occasionally. Add garlic and mushrooms, cook 10 minutes.

4 Add mushroom mixture to sauce, reheat. Add soyaroni. Pour into shallow ovenproof dish. Combine breadcrumbs and Parmesan, sprinkle on top. Bake in moderate oven 15 minutes, then place under griller to brown before serving.

Serves 4

Vegetable Strudel

Stuffed Jacket Potato with Mushrooms and Cheese

4 large old potatoes, washed

1 tspn olive oil

1 small onion, finely chopped

1 clove garlic, crushed

250g (½lb) small mushrooms, sliced

1 tblspn slivered almonds, toasted

½ cup low fat cottage cheese

½ cup low fat plain yoghurt

1 tblspn chopped parsley

1 Prick potatoes all over with a skewer. Place potatoes slightly apart directly onto oven rack in moderate oven, bake 1 hour or until tender. Remove from oven, cut in half, scoop out the flesh leaving a 1 cm (½in) thick shell of potato. Brush potatoes inside and out with oil, bake in hot oven 10 minutes.

2 Heat oil in pan, cook onion 5 minutes, stirring occasionally, add garlic and mushrooms, cook 5 minutes, stirring occasionally. Toast almonds in oven tray in moderate oven 5 minutes. Remove from heat, add toasted almonds and remaining ingredients and mashed potato. Mix well.

3 Spoon filling into potatoes on oven tray, bake in moderate oven 15 minutes or until heated through.

Serves 4

Pancakes with Artichokes, Avocado and Pinenuts

1¼ cup skim milk

¾ cup wholemeal flour

2 egg whites

1 tblspn oil

400g (13oz) can artichokes, drained, chopped

1 avocado, chopped

2 tblspn pinenuts, toasted

½ cup low fat cottage cheese

4 spring onions (scallion), chopped

1 tblspn grated Parmesan cheese

1 Combine skim milk, flour, egg whites and oil, beat well. Heat small pan, brush with oil, pour 2-3 tablespoons pancake batter into pan. Turn pancake when browned underneath, brown other side. Repeat until all batter is used up. Makes about 8 pancakes.

2 Combine artichokes, avocado, cottage cheese and spring onions in bowl.

3 Divide mixture between pancakes, roll up. Place on tray, sprinkle with Parmesan cheese, heat in moderate oven 10 minutes.

Serves 4

Sweet and Sour Tofu

250g (½lb) tofu (soy bean curd), cut into 2.5cm (1in) cubes

1 tblspn olive oil

1 red capsicum (pepper), cut into thin strips

2 carrots, cut into thin strips

155g (5oz) snowpeas

2 tspn grated ginger

1 clove garlic, crushed

1 cup pineapple chunks (fresh or canned, unsweetened)

⅓ cup water

1 cup pineapple juice

1 tblspn cornflour

1 tblspn vinegar

1 Heat oil in pan, cook tofu cubes until golden brown. Remove from pan.

2 Add red capsicum to pan with carrots, snowpeas, ginger and garlic. Cook 3 minutes.

3 Add pineapple juice, water, combined cornflour and vinegar. Cook until mixture boils and thickens.

4 Return tofu to pan, cook until heated through.

Serves 4

Sweet and Sour Tofu

Vegetable Pizza

WHOLEMEAL CRUST:

¾ cup wholemeal plain flour

½ tspn sugar

½ tspn salt

½ x 7g (¼oz) sachet dried yeast

1 tblspn olive oil

¼ cup hot water

TOPPING:

2 tblspn tomato paste

½ cup low fat cottage cheese

1 onion, sliced

1 red capsicum (pepper), sliced

60g (2oz) small mushrooms, sliced

1 tblspn black olives

1 tspn dried oregano and basil

1 tblspn grated Parmesan cheese

1 To make wholemeal crust: Sift flour, sugar and salt into bowl, add yeast. Make well in centre, add combined oil and water, mix to a firm dough, turn onto floured surface, knead for 10 minutes or until smooth and elastic. Place in lightly oiled bowl, cover, stand in warm place 30 minutes or until doubled in bulk. Knead dough until smooth.

2 Roll out dough large enough to line 28cm (11 in) pizza pan.

3 Spread tomato paste evenly over dough. Cover with cottage cheese. Arrange onion, capsicum and mushrooms over cottage cheese. Sprinkle with olives, herbs and Parmesan cheese. Bake in hot oven 20 minutes.

Serves 4

SATISFYING SALADS

With the variety of wonderful fruit and vegetables available, salads can be delightful, satisfying main meals. These crisp and tasty dishes are packed full of health and goodness.

Chicken Salad with Minted Cucumber Dressing

2 whole chicken breasts, skinned, boned, halved

1 carrot

1 small onion

6 peppercorns

DRESSING:

2 tblspn non fat yoghurt

2 tblspn reduced kilojoule mayonnaise

1 clove garlic, crushed

2 tspn finely chopped mint

⅓ cup chopped cucumber

1 Remove any visible fat from chicken.

2 In a saucepan combine chicken, carrot, onion and peppercorns. Add water to cover, season with a little salt, bring to a boil.

3 Reduce heat, simmer until chicken is cooked through. Strain. Reserve broth for soup. Discard carrot, onion and peppercorns. Cut chicken into 2.5cm (1in) cubes. Set aside to cool.

4 To make dressing: Combine yoghurt, mayonnaise, garlic, mint and cucumber in a bowl. Add cooled chicken. Toss to coat. Serve immediately or refrigerate until ready to eat.

Serves 4

Salad Nicoise

2 large potatoes, peeled

2 cups green beans, tips removed and cut in half

2 hard-boiled eggs, peeled and sliced (See note)

¼ cup black olives

2 tblspn capers, drained

8 tinned anchovy fillets, drained

440g (14oz) can red salmon, bones removed and drained

2 tblspn lemon juice

1 garlic clove, crushed

1 tblspn chopped fresh basil

½ cup safflower oil

1 Cook potatoes until tender, cut into bite-size pieces and set aside.

2 Bring a medium saucepan of water to the boil, add beans, cook for 1 minute, strain and refresh with cold water and set aside.

3 In a large bowl combine potatoes, beans, eggs, olives, capers, anchovy fillets and salmon.

4 Mix together lemon juice, garlic, basil and oil and toss through salad.

Note: Remember, on a low cholesterol diet you should not eat more than 2 egg yolks in a week. Egg whites contain no cholesterol.

Serves 4

Salad Nicoise

Ceviche Salad

Ceviche Salad

32 scallops, rinsed and deveined

½ cup lemon juice

¼ cup lime juice

2 tspn fresh oregano, chopped

1 large red onion, peeled and sliced

1 capsicum (pepper), seeds removed, chopped

radicchio leaves

1 small cucumber, finely sliced

¼ cup safflower oil

1 tblspn chopped fresh coriander

1 Rinse and drain scallops, toss in combined lemon and lime juice. Add oregano, onion and capsicum, cover and refrigerate overnight.

2 Arrange radicchio lettuce leaves on serving plates.

3 Remove scallops with a slotted spoon, reserve marinade and place scallops onto lettuce bed. Arrange cucumber slices in salad.

4 Mix the marinade with the oil and coriander and pour over salad.

Serves 4

Macaroni and Turkey Salad

A perfect way to use leftover Christmas turkey

1⅓ cups cooked elbow macaroni, cooled

1⅓ cups diced cooked turkey

4 zucchini (courgettes), thinly sliced

½ Spanish onion, chopped

1 carrot, thinly sliced

DRESSING:

⅓ cup reduced kilojoule mayonnaise

1 tspn Dijon mustard

1 tspn lemon juice

1 In a salad bowl combine macaroni, turkey, zucchini, onion and carrot.

2 To make dressing: Whisk all ingredients in a small bowl until well combined.

3 Add dressing to salad bowl, toss well to combine. Cover, refrigerate at least 1 hour before serving.

Serves 4

Creamy Dressing

½ cup low fat cottage cheese

2 tblspn safflower oil

2 tblspn freshly squeezed lemon juice

2 tblspn dry white wine

2 tspn Dijon mustard

½ tspn dried French tarragon

freshly ground white pepper

1 Place cottage cheese in a processor. Blend until smooth. Add remaining ingredients, process until well combined. Allow ¼ cup per person.

Makes 1 cup

Chicken and Orange Salad

Chicken and Orange Salad

2 cups cooked, skinless, chicken breast, cut into bite-size pieces

½ cup celery, sliced

½ cup water-chestnuts, cut in halves

1 cup orange segments

1 medium red onion, finely chopped

1 tblspn fresh parsley

⅓ cup safflower oil

1 small garlic clove, crushed

3 tblspn tarragon vinegar

1 Gently combine chicken with the celery, water-chestnuts, orange segments and onion.

2 Combine parsley, oil, garlic and tarragon vinegar in a jar, shake well and pour over salad.

Serves 4

Sirloin Steak Salad

315g (10oz) sirloin steak, grilled, cut into julienne

2 red capsicum (peppers), cut into julienne

2 spring onions (scallions), sliced into strips

½ onion, sliced into half rings

¼ cup vinaigrette (see page 24)

freshly ground black pepper

butter lettuce leaves

1 orange, peeled, segmented

1 cup button mushrooms, sliced

4 cherry tomatoes

1 Combine beef, capsicum, spring onion and onion in a bowl. Add dressing, toss to mix well. Season to taste with freshly ground black pepper.

2 Place lettuce leaves on 4 plates. Arrange beef in the centre, surround with orange segments, mushrooms and tomato. Serve immediately.

Serves 4

Tuna and Pear Salad with Curry Dressing

3 x 185g (6oz) cans water-packed tuna, drained

⅓ cup unpeeled diced pear

lettuce leaves

DRESSING:

⅓ cup reduced kilojoule mayonnaise

2 tblspn non fat yoghurt

1½ tspn mild curry powder

1 Divide tuna into chunks. Combine in a salad bowl with pear.

2 To make dressing: Combine mayonnaise, yoghurt and curry powder in a small bowl. Whisk until smooth.

3 Pour dressing over tuna and pear, toss well to coat. Serve on lettuce leaves.

Serves 4

Chicken and Rice Salad with Mustard Dressing

2¾ cups water

1 cup long grain rice

salt

1 whole cooked chicken breast, boned, skin and all visible fat removed, cut into cubes

½ red capsicum (pepper), cubed

¼ cup sliced spring onions (scallion)

2 tblspn chopped green olives

DRESSING:

2 tblspn olive oil

2 tblspn white wine vinegar

1 tblspn Dijon mustard

1 Bring water to a boil, add rice and a little salt. Reduce heat to a simmer, cook about 20 minutes or until all water has been absorbed and rice is tender. Place rice in a bowl.

2 To make dressing: Place oil, vinegar and mustard in a screwtop jar, shake until well combined.

3 Mix dressing into rice while still warm.

4 Add chicken, capsicum, spring onion and olives to bowl, toss well to combine. Serve at room temperature.

Serves 4

Vinaigrette

¼ cup safflower oil

½ cup red wine vinegar

3 cloves garlic, bruised with the blade of a knife

½ tspn freshly ground black pepper

1 Combine all ingredients in a screwtop jar, shake until well combined. Allow 1 tablespoon per person. Leave garlic cloves in the jar until the dressing is finished. Keep refrigerated.

Makes ¾ cup

Herbed Seafood Salad

24 cooked scallops, deveined

24 cooked king prawns (shrimp), shelled and deveined

4 tblspn vinegar

¼ cup lime juice

3 tblspn orange juice

1 garlic clove, lightly crushed

1 red chilli, seeds removed, finely sliced

2 tblspn green capsicum (pepper), cut into fine short strips

¼ cup stuffed green olives, cut into halves

2 tblspn chopped fresh coriander

¼ cup safflower oil

1 Combine scallops and prawns with vinegar, lime juice, orange juice and garlic, cover and chill for 2 hours.

2 Strain scallops and prawns, reserve marinade. Add chilli, capsicum, olives and coriander to scallops and prawns, toss well.

3 Mix oil into reserved marinade and pour dressing over salad. Garnish with lemon slices if desired.

Serves 8

Pawpaw (Papaya) filled with Seafood Salad in a Creamy Dressing

250g (½lb) barramundi

250g (½lb) prawns (shrimp), shelled, deveined, tails left intact

Creamy Dressing (recipe follows)

2 ripe pawpaws (papayas)

2 kiwifruit

4 spring onions (scallions), chopped

Cos lettuce leaves

watercress sprigs to garnish

1 Plunge barramundi in 4 cups boiling water, reduce heat, simmer about 10 minutes, or until fish is cooked through. Remove with slotted spoon, cool in iced water.

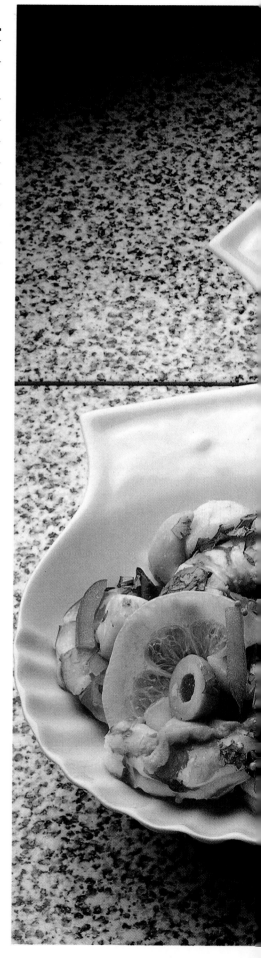

Herbed Seafood Salad

2 Add prawns to simmering water, cook until they have changed colour, about 5 minutes. Drain, cool in iced water.

3 Cut barramundi into bite-size pieces, combine with prawns in a bowl. Toss with dressing, cover, refrigerate overnight.

4 Halve pawpaws, remove flesh. Make sure to keep shells intact. Cut flesh into 2cm (¾in) cubes. Cut kiwifruit into slices. Add pawpaw cubes, kiwifruit and spring onions to barramundi and prawns, toss gently.

5 Spoon into halved pawpaw shells, place on lettuce leaves. Decorate with watercress sprigs. Serve immediately.

Serves 4

Chef's Salad with Chicken

155g (5oz) green beans, topped and tailed

155g (5oz) carrots, cut into 1cm (½in) diagonal slices

155g (5oz) cauliflower, divided into flowerets

4 spring onions (scallions), sliced

240g (8oz) can artichoke hearts, drained, halved

6 fresh mushrooms, cleaned, sliced

½ cup vinaigrette (recipe follows)

½ Cos lettuce, torn into bite-size pieces

375g (¾lb) grilled skinless chicken breast, cut into strips

1 cup cooked peas

12 cherry tomatoes

1 Cook, steam or microwave beans, carrots and cauliflower separately until just tender. Drain, cool.

2 Combine cooled vegetables with spring onions, artichoke hearts and mushrooms. Add vinaigrette, toss well, refrigerate 1 hour.

3 In a salad bowl combine lettuce, chicken and peas. Add marinated vegetables, toss to combine. Add cherry tomatoes, toss again. Serve immediately, 1½ cup per person.

Serves 6

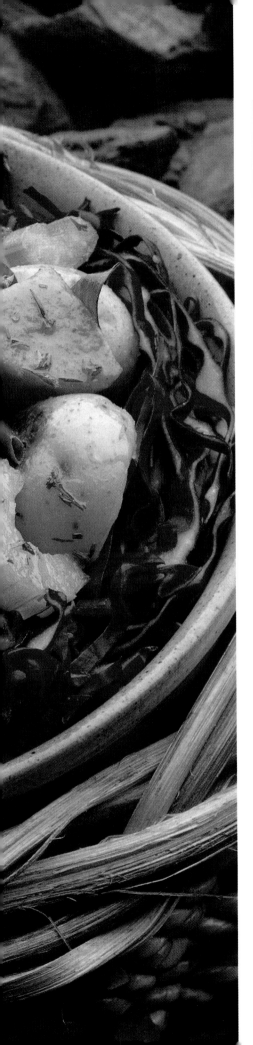

> *When choosing oil look for the polyunsaturated type, e.g., safflower oil and the monounsaturated type, e.g., olive oil. These can actually lower your blood cholesterol levels. Current medical research indicates that safflower oil is preferable for most cooking purposes, however if you really want the good taste and flavour of olive oil, this is all right in moderation.*

Fried Potato Salad with Dill Dressing

2 tblspn safflower oil

250g (½lb) baby new potatoes, halved

1 large orange sweet potato, peeled, cut into 2.5cm (1in) cubes

2 sticks celery, chopped

4 spring onions (scallions), finely chopped

½ small red cabbage, finely shredded

DILL DRESSING:

½ cup French dressing

1 tblspn chopped parsley

1 tblspn French mustard

1 tblspn chopped dill

1 Heat oil in large pan, add potatoes, cook until potatoes are lightly browned and just tender, drain on absorbent paper.

2 Combine potatoes in bowl with celery and spring onions. Add dressing, toss gently. Arrange salad on bed of shredded red cabbage.

3 To make dill dressing: Combine all ingredients in a jar, shake well. Serve warm or cold.

Serves 4

Beetroot, Artichoke and Avocado Salad

225g (7oz) can sliced beetroot, drained

400g (13oz) can artichoke hearts, drained, halved

1 avocado, coarsely chopped

⅓ cup pecan halves

4 spring onions (scallions), finely chopped

1 cup alfalfa sprouts

DRESSING:

1 tblspn olive oil

1 tblspn walnut oil

1 tblspn white wine vinegar

½ tspn French mustard

1 clove garlic, crushed

1 Combine beetroot, artichokes, avocado, pecans and spring onions in bowl, add dressing, toss well.

2 Arrange sprouts on serving plates, top with beetroot mixture.

3 Combine all ingredients for dressing in a jar, shake well.

Serves 4

Fried Potato Salad with Dill Dressing

Red Pasta Salad with Italian Dressing

500g (1lb) red fettucine

125g (4oz) small snowpeas

125g (4oz) small mushrooms, sliced

1 small red capsicum (pepper), cut into small strips

230g (7½oz) sliced water chestnuts, drained

2 tempeh burgers, cut into small strips

1 tblspn black olives

ITALIAN DRESSING:

¼ cup olive oil

¼ cup lemon juice

1 clove garlic, crushed

1 Cook pasta in large pot of rapidly boiling water, boil rapidly, uncovered 5 minutes, drain. Combine pasta with dressing in bowl.

2 Steam snowpeas 1 minute, drain, cool under cold running water. Add to pasta with mushrooms, capsicum, water chestnuts and tempeh strips.

3 To make dressing: Combine all ingredients in jar, shake well.

Serves 4

Tomato, Bocconcini and Basil Salad

4 tomatoes, halved

1 mignonette lettuce, washed

2 bocconcini, sliced (See note)

2 spring onions (scallions), finely chopped

8 basil leaves

2 tblspn olive oil

1 tblspn red wine vinegar

1 clove garlic, crushed

1 tspn sugar

1 Arrange tomato halves on bed of lettuce. Top each half with a basil leaf and a slice of bocconcini. Sprinkle with spring onions.

2 Combine remaining ingredients in a jar, shake well. Drizzle dressing over tomatoes.

Serves 4

Green Vegetable and Pasta Salad

Green Vegetable and Pasta Salad

250g (½lb) dried green pasta spirals

1 tspn olive oil

1 cup green peas

125g (4oz) green beans, halved

1 cup broccoli flowerets

2 small zucchini (courgette), sliced diagonally

2 tblspn almonds

⅓ cup olive oil

2 tblspn freshly squeezed lemon juice

1 tspn French mustard

2 tspn chopped tarragon (preserved in vinegar, available from delicatessens)

1 Cook pasta in boiling water until tender, drain, rinse under cold water and drain again. Place pasta in large bowl. Add oil, toss well.

2 Bring large pan of water to the boil. Add vegetables, count to 30, drain. Rinse under cold water, drain again. Add to pasta.

3 To toast almonds on oven tray, bake in moderate oven 5 minutes, cool.

4 Combine oil, lemon juice, mustard and tarragon, add to salad with almonds. Refrigerate 2 hours before serving.

Serves 4

Avocado Sushi

2 cups short grain rice

3 cups water

5 sheets nori (see note)

⅓ cup rice vinegar

⅓ cup sugar

3 tspn salt

2 tspn wasabi paste (see note)

1 small green cucumber, peeled, seeded, cut into thin strips

1 avocado, peeled, cut into thin strips

60g (2oz) packet sliced pickled ginger, cut into thin strips. (see note)

1 Combine rice and water in pan, bring to boil, reduce heat, simmer, uncovered until water is absorbed. Cover pan, simmer 5 minutes.

2 Stir in combined vinegar, sugar and salt. Arrange nori sheets in single layer on oven tray. Toast in moderate oven 2 minutes or until crisp.

3 Cut a strip about 4cm (1½in) wide from the narrow end of the nori sheet. Place the large piece of nori in the centre of a bamboo mat, place the extra narrow strip in the centre; this helps strengthen the nori during rolling.

4 Spread about a fifth of the rice over nori. At the end furthest away from you leave a 4cm (1½in) edge. Make a hollow with (wet) fingers horizontally across the centre. Spread the wasabi past along hollow in rice. Place a combination of cucumber, avocado and ginger in hollow of rice.

5 Use bamboo mat to help roll the sushi, pressing firmly as you roll. Remove bamboo mat. Use a sharp knife to cut sushi into 4cm (1½in) slices.

Serves 4

Note: Nori, wasabi paste and pickled ginger are available from Asian food shops.

Cottage Cheese and Fruit with Orange Dressing

400g (13oz) low fat cottage cheese

½ tspn grated orange rind

1 orange, segmented

¼ cup pecan halves

1 mignonette lettuce, washed

1 stick celery, sliced

1 red Delicious apple, thinly sliced

ORANGE DRESSING:

¼ cup olive oil

1½ tblspn red wine vinegar

1 tspn sugar

¼ tspn basil and tarragon

1 Combine cottage cheese with orange rind and half the orange segments. Toast pecan nuts on oven tray in moderate oven 5 minutes. Add to cottage cheese mixture.

2 Place lettuce on serving plates, top with cheese mixture. Serve with remaining orange, celery and apple. Top with Dressing.

3 To make dressing: Combine all ingredients in jar, shake well.

Serves 4

Fried Brown Rice Salad

1½ cups brown rice

1 tblspn olive oil

1 onion, sliced

1 clove garlic, crushed

250g (½lb) small mushrooms, sliced

1 large carrot, coarsely grated

125g (4oz) small snowpeas

4 spring onions (scallions), chopped

¼ cup roasted cashew nuts

DRESSING:

1½ tblspn brown vinegar

1 tspn soy sauce

½ tspn sesame oil

1 Cook rice in large pot of boiling water, boil rapidly, uncovered, 30 minutes; drain, rinse under cold water, drain.

2 Heat oil in large pan, add onion, cook 5 minutes or until golden, stirring occasionally. Add garlic, mushrooms, carrot and snowpeas, stir-fry until snowpeas are just tender.

3 Add spring onions, rice, cashew nuts and dressing, stir-fry until rice is heated through. Serve warm or cold.

4 To make dressing: Combine all ingredients in a jar, shake well.

Serves 4

Tofu and Pinenut Salad with Curry Dressing

½ cup pinenuts

1 cos lettuce

6 spring onions (scallions), chopped

4 slices wholemeal bread, crusts removed and chopped

1 mango, sliced

1 tblspn chopped parsley

1 tblspn chopped basil

200g (6½oz) silken tofu (soy bean curd), cut into 1cm (½in) cubes

DRESSING:

⅓ cup oil

2 tblspn vinegar

2 tspn curry powder

1 tspn honey

1 Toast pinenuts on oven tray in moderate oven for about 5 minutes, cool.

2 Combine pinenuts, roughly torn lettuce and spring onions in bowl.

3 Toast bread cubes on oven tray in moderate oven for aboout 10 minutes, cool.

4 Add toasted bread cubes to salad with mango, parsley, basil and tofu. Toss gently. Pour dressing over.

5 To make dressing: Combine all ingredients in a jar, shake well.

Serves 4

Chickpea Salad with Tzatziki Dressing

2 x 410g (13oz) can chickpeas, drained

2 tomatoes, chopped

1 green capsicum (pepper), cut into small strips

1 yellow capsicum (pepper), cut into small strips

TZATZIKI DRESSING:

2 tblspn olive oil

1 tblspn cider vinegar

2 tblspn low fat plain yoghurt

1 tspn French mustard

2 cloves garlic, crushed

1 tspn sugar

1 Combine chickpeas, tomatoes and capsicum in a bowl. Add dressing, mix well.

2 Combine all ingredients for dressing in a jar, shake well.

Serves 4

Tofu and Pinenut Salad with Curry Dressing

PASTA, RICE AND PULSES

These staple foods are major sources of complex carboydrate, dietary fibre, protein, minerals and vitamins. Try these flavoursome dishes for energy and health.

Pesto with Spaghetti

2 cups fresh chopped basil leaves

⅓ cup safflower oil

3 tblspn pinenuts

4 garlic cloves, crushed

½ tspn sugar

¼ tspn salt

375g (¾lb) dry spaghetti

1 In a blender or food processor blend basil, oil, pinenuts, garlic, sugar and salt until ingredients are evenly blended, cover and set aside.

2 Bring a large saucepan of water to the boil. Add the spaghetti and cook until just tender, approximately 8 minutes.

3 Drain and toss pesto through until evenly coated.

Serves 6

Thai Noodle Salad

125g (4oz) dried Chinese noodles

1 cup chopped cucumber

½ cup shredded spring onion (scallion)

¼ cup carrot matchsticks

½ cup alfalfa sprouts

¼ cup chopped fresh coriander

SAUCE:

2 tblspn safflower oil

2 tblspn mild soy sauce

2 tblspn tahini

2 cloves garlic, crushed

1 tspn chilli flakes

1 Cook noodles in boiling water until tender, about 3 minutes. Drain. Cool. Refrigerate 30 minutes.

2 In a very small frying pan heat oil, add to soy sauce, tahini, garlic and chilli flakes. Mix well.

3 Place chilled noodles in a salad bowl, add cucumber, spring onion, carrot, sprouts and coriander. Add sauce, mix well. Cover, refrigerate at least 1 hour. Serve chilled.

Serves 4

Pesto with Spaghetti

Pilau with Apricots and Sultanas

1 tblspn margarine

2 tblspn slivered almonds

1 clove garlic, crushed

2 tblspn chopped onion

½ tspn grated fresh ginger

½ tspn salt

1 clove

2.5cm (1in) cinnamon stick

½ tspn turmeric

¾ cup long-grain rice

2 scant cups water

1½ tblspn chopped dried apricots

1 tblspn sultanas

1 Melt margarine in a casserole, add almonds, saute until golden. Add garlic, onion and ginger, saute until onion is golden, about 5 minutes.

2 Add salt, clove, cinnamon and turmeric. Mix well. Add rice, stir to coat.

3 Add water, bring to a boil, reduce heat to a simmer, cover. Cook about 25 minutes, or until all water has been absorbed.

4 Stir in apricots and sultanas, fluffing rice. Serve hot, ½ cup per person.

Serves 6

Shells with Sate Sauce

1½ cups pasta shells

1 tblspn chopped fresh coriander

SAUCE:

⅓ cup crunchy peanut butter

1 tblspn chopped spring onions (scallions)

2 tspn sesame oil

2 tspn white wine vinegar

¼ tspn chilli flakes

1 Boil pasta in very lightly salted boiling water until al dente. Drain.

2 Meanwhile combine peanut butter, spring onions, oil, vinegar and chilli flakes in a bowl. Mix well.

3 Combine sauce with hot pasta. Toss well to coat. Serve hot, or refrigerate to serve chilled, garnished with coriander.

Serves 4

Barley and Tomato Casserole with Olives

1 cup barley

1 cup water

2 tblspn safflower oil

2½ cups chopped tomato

¼ cup dry white wine

3 tblspn tomato paste

1 large onion, peeled and chopped

½ cup stuffed green olives, halved

1 Soak barley in water for 2 hours, drain well.

2 Heat oil in a large frying pan over medium heat. Add the barley and cook, stirring constantly for 10 minutes.

3 Add the tomato, wine and tomato paste and simmer for 20 minutes.

4 Add onion and cook further 5 minutes. Mix through olives and serve immediately.

Serves 8

Barley and Tomato Casserole with Olives

Wild Rice Casserole

¼ cup chopped onion

1/8 tspn chilli flakes

pinch of thyme

1 bay leaf

2 cups degreased chicken stock

½ cup wild rice

½ cup brown rice

⅓ cup chopped onion, extra

1 tblspn dry white wine

125g (4oz) button mushrooms, sliced

1 spring onion (scallion), sliced

1 tblspn freshly squeezed lemon juice

1 tblspn Dijon mustard

½ red capsicum (pepper), seeded, chopped

1 In a saucepan combine onion, chilli flakes, thyme and bay leaf with chicken stock. Bring to a boil, add wild and brown rice. Return to a boil, reduce heat to a simmer, cover, cook 45 minutes. Drain thoroughly.

2 Meanwhile, in a frying pan saute extra onion in wine until transparent, about 5 minutes. Add mushrooms, spring onions and lemon juice. Saute 2 minutes. Add mustard, mix in well.

3 Combine rice, mushroom mixture and capsicum. Spoon into a greased casserole, cover, cook in a 160°C (325°F) oven until heated through, about 30 minutes. Serve hot, ½ cup per person.

Serves 6

Spaghetti with Asparagus

250g (½lb) spaghetti

500g (1lb) asparagus, sliced diagonally into 2.5cm (1in) pieces

salt

pepper

SAUCE:

2 tblspn olive oil

1 tblspn Dijon mustard

¼ cup chopped Spanish onion

1 clove garlic, finely chopped

½ tspn anchovy paste

2 tblspn chopped parsley

1 tblspn chopped fresh basil

1 To make sauce: Combine oil, mustard, onion, garlic, anchovy paste, parsley and basil in a bowl. Whisk until smooth. Set aside.

2 Boil spaghetti in lightly salted boiling water until al dente, drain, reserve ½ cup cooking liquid.

3 Meanwhile cook asparagus in boiling water until barely tender, about 3 minutes. Drain.

4 Toss pasta with sauce, mix in asparagus. A little of the cooking water can be added if dish seems too dry. Season to taste with salt and freshly ground black pepper. Serve hot.

Serves 4

Fettucine Alfredo

155g (5oz) fettucine

SAUCE:

1 clove garlic

¾ cup low fat cottage cheese

2 tblspn grated Parmesan cheese

1 Add fettucine to a large pot of very lightly salted boiling water. Cook until fettucine is al dente. Drain.

2 Meanwhile, make sauce: With machine running add garlic clove to processor. Chop finely. Add cottage cheese and Parmesan, blend until smooth.

3 In a heated bowl combine fettucine with sauce, toss well. Serve hot.

Serves 4

Marinated Bean Salad

1 cup canned red kidney beans, rinsed and drained

1 cup canned chickpeas, rinsed and drained

1 cup canned pinto beans, rinsed and drained

1 cup green beans, blanched

2 zucchini (courgette), blanched and sliced into strips

1 carrot, blanched and sliced into strips

½ cup water-chestnuts, drained

2 pimentos, sliced into strips

2 tblspn chopped fresh parsley

1 tblspn chopped fresh basil

½ cup Italian dressing

1 Combine red kidney beans, chickpeas, pinto beans, green beans, zucchini, carrot, chestnuts, pimentos, parsley, basil and Italian dressing in a large bowl.

2 Toss well, cover and refrigerate 4 to 6 hours. Toss again before serving, serve chilled.

Serves 6

Marinated Bean Salad

Pearl Barley with Vegetables

½ cup chopped onion

¼ cup chopped celery

2 tblspn margarine

½ cup chopped mushrooms

1 cup pearl barley

2 cups degreased chicken stock

salt

1 In a saucepan saute onion and celery in margarine until onion is golden, about 5 minutes. Add mushrooms, saute a further 3 minutes.

2 Add barley. Mix well. Add 1 cup of the chicken stock, season to taste with salt, bring to a boil. Reduce heat, cover, simmer 25 minutes.

3 Add remaining stock, simmer a further 25 minutes, until all liquid has been absorbed. Fluff with a fork. Serve hot.

Serves 6

Confetti Rice

½ cup long-grain rice

1¼ cup water

pinch of salt

1 tblspn olive oil

2 tinned anchovies, drained, chopped

½ red capsicum (pepper), cut into 0.5cm (¼in) cubes

1 tblspn chopped artichoke hearts

4 green olives, stoned, chopped

1 Pour rice into boiling salted water. Cover, reduce heat to a simmer. Cook about 25 minutes, or until all the water has been absorbed.

2 Add oil, anchovies, capsicum, artichoke and olives. Mix well. Place in a serving dish, cool to room temperature. Serve ½ cup per person.

Serves 4

Risotto with Green Vegetables

1 tblspn safflower oil

1 small onion, peeled and chopped

⅔ cup white rice

¼ cup dry white wine

1½ cups water

2 tblspn chopped fresh parsley

½ cup blanched broccoli flowerets

½ cup blanched chopped asparagus

½ cup blanched green peas

1 Heat the oil in a large frying pan, add the onion and cook for 3 minutes.

2 Stir in the rice and wine, cook until wine is absorbed.

3 Add water, bring to the boil, cover and cook rice until tender and liquid is absorbed, approximately 20 minutes.

4 Stir vegetables into rice and serve immediately.

Serves 4

Red Lentil and Rice Pilaf

1 cup Red Lentil and Rice Pilaf Mix (recipe follows)

3 cups degreased chicken stock or water

1 Combine mix and chicken stock or water in a saucepan, bring to boil, reduce heat to a simmer, cover. Cook about about 55 minutes, or until grains are tender. Serve hot, ½ cup per person.

Serves 6

Red Lentil and Rice Pilaf Mix

2 cups red lentils

1½ cups brown rice

1½ cups wild rice

1 cup barley

1½ cups chopped dried mushrooms

¼ cup dried parsley flakes

¼ cup dried chopped vegetables

2 tblspn dried onion flakes

2 tblspn Italian herb seasoning

1 tblspn garlic flakes

½ tpsn paprika

a pinch of celery seed

a pinch of chilli poweder

a pinch of dry mustard

1 Place lentils, brown and wild rice in a colander, rinse thoroughly under cold running water, drain.

2 Spread on a baking sheet, dry in a 150°C (300°F) oven for about 15 minutes, stirring frequently. Remove from oven, cool.

3 Place all remaining ingredients in a large bowl, mix well. Add cooled lentils and rice, stir to blend. Store in airtight containers, keeps indefinitely.

Makes 8 cups

Risotto with Green Vegetables

Pasta with Tomato and Onion Sauce

1 tblspn safflower oil

1 onion, peeled and finely chopped

2 garlic cloves, crushed

425g (13½oz) can peeled tomatoes in juice

1 tblspn sugar

315g (10oz) dry noodles or macaroni

1 Heat the oil in a medium frying pan over low heat. Add the onion and garlic, cook until transparent.

2 Add the tomatoes and their juice, basil and sugar, cook for 5 minutes, stirring occasionally.

3 Bring a large saucepan of water to the boil, add the noodles and cook until tender, approximately 8 minutes.

4 Drain the noodles and toss through the tomato onion sauce.

Serves 6

Spaghetti with Vegetables in a Cream Sauce

¾ cup broccoli flowerets

¾ cup French beans, cut into 2.5cm (1in) lengths

¼ cup sliced zucchini (courgette)

¾ cup sliced peeled carrots

185g (6oz) spaghetti

SAUCE:

1 cup low fat cottage cheese

½ cup skim milk

2 tblspn chopped fresh basil

1 Steam broccoli, beans, zucchini and carrots until tender. Cool.

2 Cook spaghetti in very lightly salted boiling water until al dente, drain, cool.

3 Puree cottage cheese in a food processor, add milk and basil, process until well blended.

4 Place cooled vegetables in a salad bowl, add pasta, toss to combine. Add sauce, toss to coat. Serve at room temperature.

Serves 4

Tabouli

½ cup finely crushed bulgur

1 small cucumber, seeded, cut into 0.5cm (¼in) cubes

2 small tomatoes, seeded, cut into 1cm (½in) pieces

3 spring onions (scallions), chopped

2 tblspn finely chopped mint

4 cups chopped parsley

DRESSING:

juice of 1 lemon

1 clove garlic, bruised with blade of a knife.

3 tspn olive ol

1 Rinse bulgur under cold running water, drain, stand.

2 To make dressing: Combine all ingredients in a screwtop jar, shake well. Stand at least 1 hour.

3 Combine cucumber, tomato, spring onions, mint and parsley in a bowl. Add bulgur, mix well.

4 Pour dressing over salad, discard garlic. Toss well to mix. Cover, refrigerate at least 2 hours. Serve cold.

Serves 4

Pasta with Tomato and Onion Sauce

Almond and Cashew Nut Roast

2 tblspn dried breadcrumbs

60g (2oz) polyunsaturated margarine

1 tblspn olive oil

1 onion, finely chopped

125g (4oz) small mushrooms, finely chopped

¼ tspn dried oregano

½ cup rolled oats

1 cup skim milk

2 egg whites, beaten

125g (4oz) cashew nuts, finely chopped

125g (4oz) almonds, finely chopped

1 Lightly oil a loaf tin, coat base and sides with breadcrumbs.

2 Heat margarine and oil in pan, add onion and mushrooms, cook, stirring, for 5 minutes. Add oregano and oats.

3 Gradually add milk, stirring continuously. Cool slightly, stir in egg whites, cashew nuts and almonds.

4 Pour into prepared loaf tin, smooth top. Bake in moderate oven 1¼ hours.

Serves 4

Vegetable Pilaf with Almonds

2 tspn olive oil

1 onion, chopped

1 clove garlic, crushed

¼ cup almonds

2 cups long grain brown rice

1 stick celery, chopped

125g (4oz) beans, chopped

125g (4oz) zucchini (courgette), chopped

125g (4oz) broccoli flowerets

1 small green capsicum (pepper), chopped

2 tblspn currants

2 tspn grated orange rind

juice of 1 orange

600ml (1pint) boiling water

1 bay leaf

1 tblspn tamari

1 Heat oil in large saucepan, cook onion 5 minutes, stirring occasionally. Add garlic, almonds and rice, cook, stirring 2 minutes.

2 Add vegetables, currants, orange rind, orange juice, water and bay leaf. Bring to the boil, simmer, covered 30 minutes or until rice is cooked.

3 Add tamari, cook covered further 5 minutes. Remove bay leaf before serving.

Serves 4

Vegetable Pilaf with Almonds

Lentil Burgers

1 cup cooked lentils

1 cup mashed potato

1 onion, finely chopped

½ cup rolled oats

¼ cup fresh wholemeal breadcrumbs

2 tspn desiccated coconut

1 tspn ground cumin

1/8 tspn chilli powder

2 egg whites, beaten

2 tblspn chopped parsley

2 tblspn lime juice

1 cup oat bran

olive oil

1 Combine all ingredients, except oat bran and oil in bowl. Form patties. Coat in oat bran.

2 Brush both sides of patties with oil. Cook under griller until golden both sides. Serve with salad.

Serves 4

Fettucine All'amatriciana

375g (¾lb) dried fettucine

2 tspn olive oil

1 onion, finely chopped

1 tspn chilli flakes

800g (26oz) can peeled tomatoes, undrained

1 tspn olive oil, extra

125g (4oz) lean leg ham, chopped

2 tblspn grated Parmesan cheese

1 Heat oil in pan, cook onion 5 minutes, stirring occasionally. Add chilli and tomatoes, simmer 5 minutes.

2 Heat extra oil in another pan, cook ham until browned.

3 Cook pasta in large pot boiling water for 5 minutes or until tender. Drain, place into large serving bowl.

4 Stir Parmesan, tomato mixture and ham through pasta. Serve immediately with green salad.

Serves 4

Cottage Pie with Lentils and Vegetables

220g (7oz) red lentils, washed

2 bay leaves

4 cups assorted chopped vegetables, such as carrots, brussel sprouts, zucchini, cauliflower, broccoli, beans, pumpkin, parsnip, celery, cabbage.

3 cups hot mashed potato (about 6 potatoes), mashed with skim milk or Shape.

2 tspn sesame seeds

¼ tspn paprika

SAUCE:

1 tspn olive oil

1 onion, finely chopped

1 clove garlic, crushed

2 cups lentil cooking stock

¼ cup tomato paste

1½ tblspn cornflour

2 tblspn water

¼ cup chopped parsley

1 Place lentils and bay leaves in pan, cover with water, bring to boil, simmer, covered 15 minutes. Drain, reserve stock for sauce. Remove bay leaves. Spread over base of a 2-litre ovenproof dish.

2 Steam (or microwave) vegetables for 5 minutes or until just tender. Place on top of lentils.

3 Spoon over sauce. Top with mashed potatoes, sprinkle with sesame seeds and paprika. Bake in moderate oven 40 minutes.

4 To make sauce: Heat oil in pan, cook onion 5 minutes, stirring occasionally. Add garlic, reserved lentil stock and tomato paste. Bring to boil, add combined cornflour and water and parsley. Cook until sauce boils and thickens, reduce heat, simmer 5 minutes.

Serves 4

Soybean Casserole

310g (10oz) can soybeans, drained

1 tblspn olive oil

½ tspn chilli powder

1 tspn grated ginger

1 clove garlic, crushed

4 spring onions (scallions), chopped

125g (4oz) mushrooms, sliced

2 sticks celery, chopped

2 carrots, chopped

225g (7oz) can water chestnuts, drained and sliced

1 tblspn cornflour

1 tblspn sherry

1 tblspn honey

1 tblspn shoyu or tamari (see note)

1 cup vegetable or degreased chicken stock

1 Heat oil in pan, add chilli, ginger and garlic, cook for 1 minute. Add vegetables and water chestnuts, cook covered 10 minutes.

2 Add combined cornflour, sherry, honey, shoyu, stock and soybeans. Stir until sauce boils and thickens, reduce heat, simmer, covered 10 minutes.

Serves 4

Note: Shoyu and tamari are available from healthfood shops.

Cottage Pie with Lentils and Vegetables

Stir-fried Chickpeas

1 cup chickpeas, soaked overnight

1 tblspn olive oil

1 onion, sliced

2 cups shredded Chinese cabbage

1 green capsicum (pepper), chopped

4 spring onions (scallions), chopped

1 clove garlic, crushed

2 tblspn tamari

2 tspn grated ginger

1 tblspn cornflour

1 cup water

1 tspn grated lemon rind

2 tblspn lemon juice

½ tspn cumin seeds

1/8 tspn chilli powder

1 Drain chickpeas. Cover with water in pan, bring to boil, reduce heat, simmer, covered 30 minutes or until tender, drain.

2 Heat oil in pan, cook onion for 5 minutes. Add cabbage, green capsicum, shallots, garlic, tamari and ginger, cook for 3 minutes.

3 Add combined cornflour and water, reserved chickpeas and remaining ingredients. Cook until mixture boils and thickens. Reduce heat, simmer, uncovered 10 minutes.

Serves 4

Tofu Stir-fry

250g (½lb) tofu

1 cup bean sprouts

2 cups boiling water

1 tblspn olive oil

1 clove garlic, crushed

1 tspn grated ginger

4 spring onions (scallions), diagonally sliced

1 small red capsicum (pepper), cut into strips

2 zucchini (courgette), sliced

1 tblspn low-salt soy sauce

1 Pour boiling water over bean sprouts, stand 2 minutes, drain.

2 Rinse tofu in hot water, drain on paper towels. Cut tofu into 2.5cm (1in) cubes.

3 Heat oil in pan, add garlic, ginger, shallots, red capsicum and zucchini, stir-fry for 5 minutes.

4 Add bean sprouts, tofu and soy sauce. Cook until heated through. Serve with rice.

Serves 4

Pasta with Avocado, Pinenuts and Ham

2 tblspn pinenuts

375g (¾lb) dried gnocchi pasta shapes

1 tblspn olive oil

125g (4oz) mushrooms, sliced

125g (4oz) lean leg ham, cut into strips (maybe less)

1 tblspn lemon juice

½ avocado, sliced

1 tblspn chopped fresh chives

2 tblspn grated Parmesan cheese

1 Place pinenuts on oven tray, bake in moderate oven or until lightly toasted, cool.

2 Cook pasta in boiling water until tender, drain.

3 Meanwhile heat oil in pan, cook mushrooms and ham 5 minutes, add lemon juice and pasta, toss well.

4 Remove from heat, add avocado, chives and pinenuts, toss gently. Serve sprinkled with Parmesan cheese.

Serves 4

Pasta with Avocado, Pinenuts and Ham

Buckwheat Noodles with Julienne Vegetables

250g (½lb) buckwheat noodles
1 tblspn olive oil
½ cup beans
1 small red capsicum (pepper)
½ cup snowpeas
1 carrot
1 clove garlic, crushed
1 tspn grated ginger
1 tspn sesame oil
1 tblspn shoyu or tamari (see note)
225g (7oz) can water chestnuts, drained and sliced
1 tblspn chopped fresh coriander

1 Cut vegetables into thin strips.

2 Heat oil in pan, stir-fry vegetables and garlic for 3 minutes. Add ginger, sesame oil, tamari and water chestnuts, cook until heated through.

3 Cook buckwheat noodles in large pot boiling water for 5 minutes or until tender, drain.

4 Divide noodles between 4 plates, top with vegetable mixture. Serve sprinkled with coriander.

Serves 4

Note: Shoyu and tamari are available at healthfood shops.

Barley Casserole

1 tblspn olive oil
125g (4oz) small mushrooms, quartered
1 stick celery, chopped
1 carrot, chopped
1 onion, chopped
1 clove garlic, crushed
1 tblspn olive oil, extra
⅔ cup pearl barley
2½ cups degreased chicken stock
2 tblspn chopped parsley

1 Heat oil in pan, cook mushrooms, celery, carrot, onion and garlic for 5 minutes, stirring occasionally. Remove from pan.

2 Heat extra oil in pan, cook barley until golden, stirring continually.

3 Combine the barley and vegetables in a casserole dish, add boiling stock then bake, covered, in moderate oven 1 hour. Serve sprinkled with parsley.

Serves 4

Tacos with Bean Filling

12 taco shells

1 avocado, sliced

2 tblspn lemon juice

½ cup low fat cottage cheese

¼ lettuce, finely shredded

1 tomato, finely chopped

1 tblspn chilli sauce (optional)

BEAN FILLING:

2 tspn olive oil

1 onion, finely chopped

45g (1½oz) pkt taco seasoning

¼ tspn chilli powder

1 red capsicum (pepper), finely chopped

1 zucchini (courgette), finely chopped

310g (10oz) can red kidney beans, drained

400g (13oz) can peeled tomatoes, undrained

¼ cup tomato paste

1 Place taco shells on oven tray. Bake in moderate oven 5 minutes.

2 Half fill taco shells with Bean Filling. Brush avocado slices with lemon juice. Top each taco with 2 teaspoons cottage cheese, some shredded lettuce, tomato, chilli sauce (if desired) and avocado slices. Serve immediately.

3 To make bean filling: Heat oil in pan, cook onion 5 minutes, stirring occasionally. Add taco seasoning and chilli powder, cook 1 minute.

4 Add red capsicum and zucchini, cook 3 minutes, stirring occasionally. Add red kidney beans, tomatoes and tomato paste. Cook 10 minutes over medium heat, stirring occasionally.

Serves 4

Bean Curry

310g (10oz) can butter beans, drained

310g (10oz) can red kidney beans, drained

1 onion, peeled

5cm (2in) piece ginger, peeled

2 cloves garlic, peeled

1 tblspn olive oil

2 tspn curry powder

1 tspn ground cumin

1 tspn turmeric

⅓ cup sweet fruit chutney

⅓ cup crunchy peanut butter

400g (13oz) can peeled tomatoes, undrained

¼ cup tomato paste

1 cup water

1 Place roughly chopped onion, ginger and garlic in processor, process until smooth.

2 Heat oil in pan, cook onion mixture, stirring occasionally, for 5 minutes, add curry, cumin and turmeric, cook, stirring, for 1 minute.

3 Add chutney, peanut butter, tomatoes, tomato paste, water and beans. Stir until well combined. Bring to boil, reduce heat, simmer, covered 20 minutes. Serve with rice and pappadams.

Serves 4

Tacos with Bean Filling

Indian Risotto with Vegetables

1 tblspn olive oil

1 onion, finely chopped

1 clove garlic, crushed

2 cups short grain brown rice

2 tblspn sunflower seeds

1 tspn curry powder, 1 tspn cumin, ¼ tspn turmeric

5 cups vegetable or degreased chicken stock

1 tblspn olive oil, extra

125g (4oz) mushrooms, sliced

2 leeks, chopped

125g (4oz) beans, chopped

½ cup low fat plain yoghurt

1 tblspn honey

2 tblspn lime juice

1 Heat oil in pan, cook onion 5 minutes, stirring occasionally. Add garlic, rice, sunflower seeds and spices. Cook, stirring constantly 3 minutes.

2 Add ½ cup boiling stock. Bring to boil, cook over medium heat until most of the stock has been absorbed, stirring occasionally.

3 Continue to add stock half a cup at a time, stirring occasionally.

4 Heat extra oil in another pan, add mushrooms, leeks and beans. Cook, stirring 5 minutes.

5 When rice is cooked, about 20 minutes, add cooked vegetables, yoghurt, honey and lime juice.

Serves 4

Ratatouille Lasagna

4 sheets instant lasagna

1 small eggplant (aubergine), thinly sliced

sea salt

2 tspn olive oil

1 onion, finely chopped

1 clove garlic, crushed

1 red capsicum (pepper), chopped

2 zucchini (courgette), chopped

400g (13oz) can tomatoes, undrained

¼ cup tomato paste

½ tspn dried basil leaves

½ tspn dried oregano leaves

½ cup low fat cottage cheese

125g (4oz) mozzarella cheese, cut into strips

1 tblspn grated Parmesan cheese

1 Spread eggplant out onto wire rack, sprinkle with salt on both sides, stand 15 minutes, then pat dry with absorbent paper.

2 Heat oil in pan, cook onion, stirring occasionally for 5 minutes. Add chopped eggplant, garlic, red capsicum, zucchini, tomatoes, tomato paste, basil and oregano. Cook, stirring occasionally 20 minutes.

3 Spread quarter of the eggplant mixture (ratatouille) over base of 20cm (8in) square dish, place two instant lasagna sheets on top, then another quarter of ratatouille, then half the cottage cheese.

4 Repeat with another quarter of ratatouille, two sheets of lasagna, remaining ratatouille, cottage cheese, Parmesan cheese and mozzarella cheese — criss cross fashion. Bake in moderate oven 35 minutes.

Serves 4

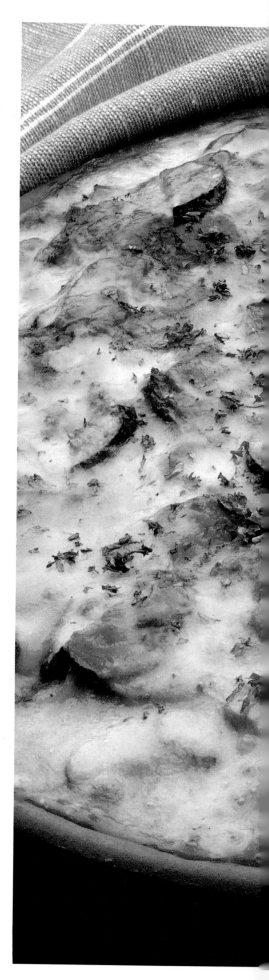

Ratatouille Lasagna

CHICKEN AND MEAT

It is important to eat moderate amounts of lean meat in a well-balanced diet, but make sure you remove all visible fat before cooking. With these delicious recipes you can add variety and good nutrition to your family meals.

Veal Casserole

500g (1lb) veal cutlets

flour

salt

pepper

1 tblspn safflower oil

1 onion, sliced

1 clove garlic, crushed

1 tblspn chopped fresh basil

¼ cup water

1 tblspn lemon juice

1 Season veal cutlets with a little salt and freshly ground black pepper. Dust with flour, shake off excess.

2 Heat oil in a casserole. When hot add cutlets. Brown on both sides. Remove, keep warm.

3 Add onion and garlic, saute until golden, about 5 minutes. Add parsley, basil, water and lemon juice. Bring to a boil, reduce heat, return veal, cover.

4 Simmer 30 minutes, add more water if necessary. Serve hot.

Serves 4

Herbed Chicken and Tomato Casserole

2 tblspn safflower oil

1 small onion, peeled and sliced

1 green capsicum (pepper), seeds removed, cut into strips

1 red capsicum (pepper), seeds removed, cut into strips

1 zucchini (courgette), sliced

1½ cups tomato puree

1 tblspn chopped fresh basil

1 tblspn chopped fresh parsley

1 tspn chopped fresh thyme

3 chicken breast fillets, 125g (4oz) each, cut into strips

1 In a large frying pan over medium heat, heat the oil and add onion. Cook until transparent.

2 Add green and red capsicum, zucchini and tomato puree. Bring to the boil, reduce heat and simmer for 10 minutes.

3 Add the basil, parsley, thyme and chicken, cook for 10 minutes or until chicken is cooked through.

Serves 4

Herbed Chicken and Tomato Casserole

Rissoles with Gravy

500g (1lb) topside mince

1 clove garlic, crushed

1 onion, chopped

1 small carrot, grated

2 tblspn wheat germ

1 tblspn chopped parsley

1 egg white

1 tspn Dijon mustard

1 tblspn safflower oil

1½ cups degreased stock

1 tblspn cornflour

1 Combine mince, garlic, onion, carrot, wheat germ, egg white, parsley and mustard. Shape into 8 balls. Place in refrigerator for 1 hour to firm.

2 Heat oil in a casserole, fry rissoles on all sides until brown. Add stock, bring to a boil, reduce heat to a simmer, cook 30 minutes.

3 Combine cornflour with 1 tablespoon cold water. Whisk into liquid, cook until mixture thickens. Serve hot.

Serves 4

Beef, Cauliflower and Snowpeas Stir-fry

125g (4oz) snowpeas

375g (12oz) fillet steak, sliced very thinly

1 tblspn safflower oil

2 tblspn chopped onion

1 clove garlic, crushed

3 cups cauliflowerets

¾ cup degreased beef stock

2 tblspn water

2 tblspn dry sherry

1½ tblspn cornflour

1 tblspn light soy sauce

2 tspn freshly grated ginger

cooked rice

1 Plunge snowpeas into boiling water. Return to a boil, cook 1 minute. Drain, refresh under cold running water. Drain again, set aside.

2 Heat oil in a frying pan. Brown beef strips. Work in 2 batches if pan seems crowded. Remove beef.

3 Add onion and garlic, saute until golden, about 5 minutes. Add cauliflowerets and stock, bring to a boil, reduce heat to medium, cook 3 minutes, stirring from time to time.

4 Combine water, sherry, cornflour, soy and ginger in a bowl. Stir into pan. Add beef strips and snowpeas.

5 Cook over medium heat until sauce thickens, stirring constantly. Serve hot with rice.

Serves 4

Skewered Lamb with Honey

¼ cup safflower oil

¼ cup unsweetened pineapple juice

¼ cup honey

1 tblspn chopped fresh dill

400g (13oz) lamb fillet, cut into 2cm (¾in) cubes

12 pineapple pieces

12 stuffed green olives, cut in halves

1 Combine oil, pineapple juice, honey and dill in a medium bowl. Add the lamb pieces, cover and refrigerate for 2 hours.

2 Thread pieces of lamb, pineapple and olives onto skewers and grill 2-3 minutes each side or until cooked.

Serves 4

Skewered Lamb with Honey

Florence Baked Chicken

4 chicken breast fillets, 125g (4oz) each

¼ cup Dijon mustard

2 tblspn white wine vinegar

1 tblspn lemon juice

3 cloves garlic

1½ tblspn chopped fresh rosemary

¾ cup fresh breadcrumbs

rosemary sprigs for garnish

1 Place chicken in a shallow baking pan, cook in a 230°C (450°F) oven until golden brown, about 15 minutes. Remove to another baking pan. Set aside. Reduce oven temperature to 140°C (275°F).

2 Pour ¾ cup hot water into baking pan used to brown chicken, scrape up any browned bits. Pour into a measuring jar, remove fat risen to the surface. Reserve broth.

3 Place mustard, vinegar, lemon juice, 2 cloves of the garlic and 1 tablespoon of the rosemary in a processor, blend until smooth. Add 2 tablespoons of the broth, blend briefly. Reserve remaining broth.

4 Pour blended mixture over chicken, bake at low temperature until cooked through, basting from time to time. This should take about 40 minutes.

5 Meanwhile, chop remaining garlic clove, combine with rosemary and the breadcrumbs. Add 2 tablespoons of the reserved chicken broth. Mix well. Spread mixture on a baking sheet, place in oven until golden and crispy.

6 Divide chicken among 4 heated plates, sprinkle with crispy crumbs, pour over any juices. Serve hot, garnished with rosemary.

Serves 4

Veal with Artichokes

2 tblspn safflower oil

1 garlic clove, crushed

½ tspn black pepper

750g (1½lb) veal fillet, cut into cubes

425 (13½oz) tin peeled tomatoes

½ cup red wine

1 cup artichoke hearts, cut in half

2 tblspn chopped fresh parsley

1 In a large frying pan, heat the oil over medium heat. Add the garlic and pepper, cook for 1 minute. Add veal and cook for 3 minutes.

2 Pour in tomatoes and wine, bring to the boil, reduce heat and simmer for 10 minutes.

3 Add the artichokes and parsley, stir until heated through.

Serves 6

Chicken Curry with Coriander Cucumber Balls

3 cucumbers, peeled

1 tblspn white vinegar

salt

2 tblspn olive oil

500g (1lb) chicken thigh fillets

1 tblspn margarine

1 onion, chopped

½ red capsicum (pepper), chopped

2 cloves garlic, crushed

2 tspn curry powder

1 Scoop out cucumber balls with a melon baller. Alternatively, cut cucumber into cubes. Place in a bowl and sprinkle with vinegar. Season very lightly with salt. Add coriander, toss well. Cover, refrigerate until ready to eat.

2 Place oil in a frying pan, saute thigh fillets until cooked through. Remove from pan, set aside.

3 Melt margarine in frying pan, add onion, capsicum and garlic, saute until vegetables are tender, about 10 minutes. Add curry powder, season to taste with salt.

4 Return chicken to pan, saute briefly to heat through and coat with sauce. Serve hot with chilled coriander cucumber balls.

Serves 6

Scaloppine al Limone (Veal with Lemon Sauce)

500g (1lb) veal scaloppine

pepper

flour

1 tblspn olive oil

1 tblspn margarine

½ cup degreased beef stock

4 lemon slices

2 tblspn freshly squeezed lemon juice

1 Pound veal slices with a mallet until very thin. Season to taste with freshly ground black pepper. Dust with flour, shake off excess.

2 Combine oil and margarine in a frying pan, heat until foaming. Add veal, saute until golden on both sides. Remove, keep warm.

3 Drain fat from pan, don't wipe. Add ⅓ cup of the stock, bring to a boil, scraping up any browned bits.

4 Reduce heat, return veal to the pan, place lemon slices on top. Cover, simmer 10 minutes, or until veal is tender.

5 Place veal on heated plates, add remaining stock to pan, reduce liquid to a glaze. Add lemon juice, cook a further minute, stirring constantly. Pour sauce over scaloppine. Serve hot.

Serves 4

Veal with Artichokes

Chicken and Capsicum (Pepper) Tortillas

TORTILLA:

1½ cups fine cornmeal

1½ cups plain flour

pinch salt

75g (2½oz) margarine, chopped

¾ cup warm water

TOPPING:

¼ cup tomato paste

100g (3½oz) low-chol cheese, grated

1 cup cooked chicken breast, chopped

2 tblspn chopped green capsicum (pepper)

2 tspn chopped red chilli

1 Mix cornmeal, flour and salt together in a medium bowl. Rub in margarine until mixture resembles fine breadcrumbs.

2 Add the water and mix to a dough. Lightly knead on a floured surface for 2 minutes.

3 Roll dough out and using a 9cm (3½in) round cutter, cut out 8 circles.

4 Place tortillas on a greased baking tray and bake in a moderate oven for 10 minutes.

5 Spread tomato paste over each tortilla, sprinkle with cheese, chicken, capsicum and chilli. Bake in a moderate oven 10 minutes.

Makes 8 to 10

Pork Chops with Herbs

2 tspn margarine

2 cloves garlic, crushed

4 pork loin chops, all visible fat removed

½ cup red wine

1 tspn chopped oregano

1 tspn chopped rosemary

1 Combine margarine and garlic, brush all over pork chops. Heat a cast iron frying pan over high heat, add pork chops, brown on both sides. Place chops on plates, keep warm.

2 Add wine, oregano and rosemary to frying pan. Bring to a boil, scraping up any browned bits. Reduce heat, simmer 5 minutes.

3 Pour juices over chops, serve hot.

Serves 4

Chicken Normandy

3 whole chicken breasts

1 tblspn olive oil

1 onion, sliced

2 Granny Smith apples, unpeeled, cored, sliced

1½ cups unsweetened apple juice

2 tblspn honey

1 tblspn calvados (optional)

1 tblspn margarine

salt

1 Remove skin and any visible fat from chicken breasts. Halve. Place in a baking dish large enough to hold breasts in one layer.

2 Place olive oil in a frying pan. Add onions, saute until golden, about 5 minutes. Add apples, saute a further minute. Arrange onions and apples over chicken.

3 In a saucepan combine apple juice, honey and calvados if used, bring to a boil. Off the heat whisk in margarine. Season to taste with salt. Pour over chicken.

4 Bake in a 180°C (350°F) oven until chicken is cooked through, about 45 minutes. Serve hot.

Serves 6

Chicken and Capsicum (Pepper) Tortillas

Chicken Keema (Curried Minced Chicken)

2 tblspn olive oil

½ green capsicum (pepper), chopped

3 garlic cloves, crushed

375g (¾lb) minced lean chicken

2 tblspn curry powder

1/8 tspn chilli powder

salt

1 cup frozen sweet corn

2 tblspn chopped fresh coriander leaves

Basmati rice (see note)

1 Heat oil in a frying pan, add capsicum and garlic, saute over moderate heat until tender, about 10 minutes.

2 Increase heat to medium high, add chicken, saute until cooked through.

3 Mix in curry and chilli powder, season lightly with salt. Add frozen corn, cook until heated through. Serve hot, sprinkled with coriander, with cooked rice.

Note: Basmati rice is available in Oriental food stores and most supermarkets.

Serves 4

Chicken Stew

4 chicken breast halves, 155g (5oz) each

½ cup sliced onion

½ cup sliced celery

1½ cups water

salt

pepper

2 cups chopped tomatoes

1 cup cooked red kidney beans

1 cup cooked sweet corn

1 tblspn tamari (see note)

1 Combine chicken, onion, celery and water in a saucepan. Add ¾ teaspoon salt and freshly ground pepper. Bring to a boil, reduce heat to a simmer. Cover, cook about 1 hour, or until chicken is tender.

2 Remove from heat, cool. Place pan with chicken and liquid in refrigerator until fat can be removed from top. Remove chicken, strain liquid. Wipe out pan.

3 Remove meat from bones, cut into chunks. Combine with strained liquid in the pan. Add tomatoes, beans and corn, heat through. Stir in tamari. Serve hot.

Note: Tamari is available in health food shops.

Serves 4

Indonesian Chicken and Green Beans

3 tblspn safflower oil

4 chicken breast fillets, 125g (4oz) each

2 cups green beans, top and tails removed, cut into 2.5cm (1in) lengths

¼ cup lemon juice

2 tblspn soy sauce

1 tblspn brown sugar

2 tspn turmeric

1 Heat oil in a large frying pan over medium heat. Cut chicken into 2cm (¾in) cubes and add to frying pan, stirring constantly until just cooked. Remove chicken from frying pan and set aside.

2 Add beans to frying pan and stir for 2 minutes. Add lemon juice, soy sauce, brown sugar, turmeric and ½ cup water.

3 Bring to the boil, simmer for 3-5 minutes, or until sauce thickens slightly. Toss chicken through beans and sauce, serve with rice if desired.

Serves 4

Indonesian Chicken and Green Beans

Steak with Tomato Mushroom Sauce

4 scotch fillet steaks, 125g (4oz) each

2 tblspn margarine

1 cup mushrooms, sliced

1 cup tomatoes, chopped

¼ cup spring onions (scallions)

1 tblspn tomato paste

1 tblspn dry white wine

1 Trim all visible fat off steaks.

2 Melt the margarine over medium heat in a large frying pan. Add the steaks and cook each side according to taste.

3 Remove steaks and add mushrooms and tomatoes to pan. Cook for 3 minutes, stir in spring onions, tomato paste and wine, cook for a further 2 minutes. Serve over steaks.

Serves 4

Warm Asian Chicken Salad

4 chicken breast fillets, 125g (4oz) each

3 cups bean sprouts

1¼ cup snowpeas

⅓ cup water chestnuts, drained, sliced

MARINADE:

¼ cup rice vinegar

1 tblspn finely chopped garlic

2 tspn soy sauce

1 tblspn sesame oil

1 To make marinade: Combine all ingredients in a screwtop jar, shake until well blended.

2 Place chicken in a bowl, pour over ¼ cup of the marinade, cover, refrigerate 24 hours, stirring from time to time.

3 Drain, grill chicken until cooked through, about 15 minutes, turning once.

4 Combine bean sprouts, snowpeas and water chestnuts, toss with remaining marinade. Divide among 4 plates, place cooked chicken on top. Serve immediately.

Serves 4

Saltimbocca (Veal with Prosciutto and Sage)

8 slices veal scaloppini, 60g (2oz) each

8 fresh sage leaves

8 very thin slices prosciutto

1 tblspn olive oil

1 tblspn margarine

½ cup dry white wine

1 Beat scaloppine until very thin. Place a sage leaf in the centre of each piece, top with a slice of prosciutto. Fasten with a toothpick.

2 Combine oil and margarine in a frying pan. When hot, add veal, prosciutto side down. Cook until lightly brown, cook other side. Altogether this should not take more than about 3-4 minutes. Remove from pan, keep warm.

3 Add wine to pan, stir over medium high heat until starting to thicken. Place veal on 4 heated plates, pour over wine sauce. Serve hot.

Serves 4

Steak with Tomato Mushroom Sauce

Skin on poultry, such as chicken and turkey, should always be removed before cooking. Once this is done, poultry has a lower fat content than most other meats. Duck and goose are too fatty for a healthy diet.
Skin on fruit and vegetables should not be removed if possible. This is a rich source of fibre and most vitamins are found just underneath the skin.

Chicken Paprika

4 chicken breast fillets

1 tblspn olive oil

1 onion, sliced

250g (½lb) small mushrooms, sliced

1 clove garlic, crushed

1 tblspn paprika

1 cup degreased chicken stock

½ cup low fat yoghurt

1 Heat oil in pan, cook onion and mushrooms 5 minutes. Add garlic and paprika, cook 1 minute, remove from pan.

2 Add chicken fillets to pan, cook on both sides until browned.

3 Return onion mixture to pan with chicken stock. Bring to boil, reduce heat, simmer 5 minutes or until chicken is just cooked.

4 Just before serving stir in yoghurt. Reheat without boiling. Serve with noodles.

Serves 4

Barbecued Marinated Chops

8 lean lamb loin chops, excess fat removed

1 tblspn olive oil

1 clove garlic, crushed

1 onion, finely chopped

¼ cup dry white wine

2 tblspn lemon juice

½ tspn dried oregano

2 bay leaves, cut in half

1 strip lemon peel

1 Place lamb chops in shallow dish in single layer. Pour over combined remaining ingredients. Turn chops to coat well. Refrigerate overnight. Turn chops occasionally.

2 Barbecue chops until brown on both sides and cooked through. Brush with marinade as they cook. Serve with jacket potatoes and salad.

Serves 4

Chicken Paprika

Pork Chops Dijon

4 lean pork loin medallions, 125g (4oz) each

1 tblspn olive oil

1 tblspn Dijon mustard

3 spring onions (scallions), chopped

2 tspn cornflour

1 cup degreased beef stock

1 tblspn chopped parsley

1 Heat oil in pan, cook pork on both sides until golden brown. Add mustard and shallots. Stir well to mix with pan juices.

2 Add combined cornflour and stock. Bring to boil, stirring continually. Cook until mixture thickens. Reduce heat and simmer for 5 minutes or until pork is tender. Serve sprinkled with parsley.

Serves 4

Glazed Rack of Lamb

4 lean racks of lamb, all visible fat removed, 155g (5oz) each

1 tspn olive oil

⅓ cup lemon juice

1 tblspn soy sauce

⅓ cup honey

2 tspn rosemary

¾ cup water

2 tblspn chopped mint

2 tblspn brown vinegar

1 tblspn sugar

2 tblspn water, extra

1 Combine oil, lemon juice, soy sauce and honey in large dish. Add racks of lamb, turn to coat well with marinade, stand for 2 hours, turning occasionally.

2 Drain racks, reserve marinade for basting. Place rack in baking dish, brush with marinade. Sprinkle with rosemary. Bake in moderate oven for 45 minutes or until just cooked. Brush frequently with pan juices.

3 After 30 minutes, pour water in to prevent juices burning on bottom of pan. Remove racks when cooked, keep warm.

4 Place baking dish on top of stove, bring to boil, cook for 5 minutes. Add mint, vinegar, sugar and extra water, bring to boil, simmer for 2 minutes. Serve racks of lamb with sauce.

Serves 4

Spiced Pork Fillet

500g (1lb) pork fillet

1 tblspn tomato sauce

1 tblspn honey

1/8 tspn five spice powder

2 tspn soy sauce

1 tblspn honey, extra

SAUCE:

½ cup chicken stock

1 tblspn dry sherry

1 tspn sugar

½ tspn oyster sauce

2 tspn cornflour

1 Marinate pork fillets in mixture of tomato sauce, honey, five spice powder and soy sauce for 30 minutes. Bake in moderate oven 20 minutes.

2 Brush fillets with extra honey on both sides, bake further 10 minutes.

3 Combine all ingredients for sauce in pan, cook until sauce boils and thickens. Cut pork into 1cm (½in) slices, serve with sauce.

Serves 4

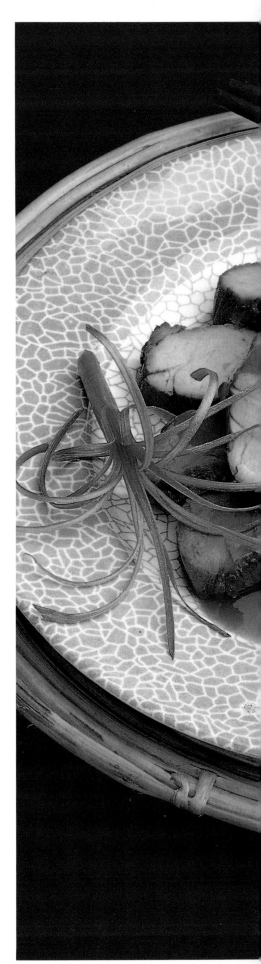

Spiced Pork Fillet

Green Peppercorn Steak

4 eye fillet steaks, all visible fat removed, 125g (4oz) each

1 tspn green peppercorns, crushed

1 tblspn olive oil

1 tblspn brandy

1 tblspn lemon juice

1 Rub steaks on both sides with crushed green peppercorns.

2 Heat oil in pan, cook steak until brown underneath, turn over and cook until browned on the other side. Add brandy and lemon juice to pan. Ignite with match. Let flames subside before serving with mustard.

Serves 4

Veal with Mushrooms and Capers

4 veal loin chops, all visible fat removed, 155g (5oz) each

1 tblspn olive oil

1 onion, finely chopped

1 clove garlic, crushed

125g (4oz) small mushrooms, sliced

1 tblspn capers

1 cup skim milk

2 tspn cornflour

3 tspn water

1 Heat oil in pan, add onions and garlic, cook for 5 minutes, add mushrooms, cook for 3 minutes or until softened. Remove from pan.

2 Cook veal in pan until brown on both sides. Add capers, skim milk and combined cornflour and water, cook until mixture boils and thickens.

3 Return onion mixture to pan, simmer, covered for 10 minutes or until veal is tender.

Serves 4

Osso Bucco

8 slices veal knuckles for osso bucco

1 tblspn olive oil

2 onions, finely chopped

2 carrots, finely chopped

2 sticks celery, finely chopped

2 cloves garlic, crushed

2 tblspn chopped fresh parsley

½ cup dry white wine

400g (13oz) can peeled tomatoes, undrained

¼ cup tomato paste

1 cup degreased chicken or veal stock

GREMOLATA GARNISH:

1 clove garlic, crushed

2 tblspn chopped fresh parsley

1 tspn grated lemon rind

1 Heat oil in pan, brown veal on both sides. Add onions, carrots, celery, garlic and parsley, cook 5 minutes.

2 Add wine and scrape base of pan with wooden spoon. Add tomatoes, tomato paste and stock. Bring to boil, simmer, cook 1 hour.

3 Sprinkle combined Gremolata ingredients over veal, cover, cook 2 minutes before serving.

Serves 4

Apricot Chicken

4 chicken breast fillets, 125g (4oz) each

2 tblspn pecan nuts, chopped

1 cup apricot nectar

4 spring onions (scallions), chopped

2 tspn wholegrain mustard

1 clove garlic, crushed

1 Arrange chicken fillets in lightly oiled shallow ovenproof dish.

2 Toast pecan nuts on oven tray in moderate oven for 5 minutes.

3 Combine apricot nectar with pecan nuts, shallots, mustard and garlic, pour over chicken. Turn chicken to coat all over.

4 Bake in moderate oven for 12 minutes or until just cooked through.

Serves 4

Pork with Apple Cider Sauce

500g (1lb) pork fillets, all visible fat removed

1 tspn olive oil

1 onion, sliced

2 Granny Smith apples, peeled, cored, sliced

1 cup unsweetened apple cider

1 tblspn pitted prunes, chopped

1 tblspn lemon juice

1 tblspn chopped parsley

1 Heat oil in pan, cook onion and apple for 5 minutes, add lemon juice.

2 Add cider and prunes, bring to boil, simmer for 5 minutes, add lemon juice.

3 Place pork fillets in lightly oiled, shallow ovenproof dish. Pour apple mixture over, bake in moderate oven for 30 minutes or until pork is just cooked, sprinkle with parsley.

4 Serve with sweet potatoes and green vegetables.

Serves 4

Osso Bucco

Stir-fried Beef and Black Bean Sauce

500g (1lb) lean beef strips

1 egg white

1 tblspn dry sherry

2 tblspn soy sauce

1 tspn cornflour

1 tblspn canned black beans

pinch sugar

⅓ cup water

2 tblspn olive oil

4 spring onions (scallions), cut diagonally into 2.5cm (1in) lengths

1 red capsicum (pepper), cut into strips

1 tspn curry powder

2 tspn cornflour, extra

1 Place beef in bowl. Pour over combined egg white, sherry, soy sauce and cornflour, mix well. Stand for 30 minutes.

2 Put beans in small dish, cover with water, stand for 15 minutes, drain, rinse under cold running water. Add sugar and one teaspoon water, mash well.

3 Heat 1 tablespoon oil in pan, add spring onions, red capsicum and curry powder, cook for 2 minutes, stirring occasionally, remove from pan.

4 Heat remaining oil in pan, add meat and marinade, cook until browned. Return vegetables to pan with bean mixture, mix well. Add combined cornflour and water, stir until mixture boils and thickens.

Serves 4

Lamb Curry

500g (1lb) lean lamb, cubed

1 onion, roughly chopped

2 cloves garlic, peeled

4cm (1½in) piece green ginger, peeled roughly chopped

2 tblspn crunchy peanut butter

2 tspn curry powder

2 tspn cumin

1 tspn curry paste

½ tspn sambal oelek

400g (13oz) can tomatoes, undrained

2 tblspn fruit chutney

1 cup water

1 Place lamb in casserole dish.

2 Place onion, garlic and ginger in processor, process until smooth. Add remaining ingredients except water, process until smooth. Add water, process until smooth.

3 Pour over lamb, mix well. Bake in a covered casserole in moderate oven for 1 hour, or until lamb is tender. Serve with rice and salad.

Serves 4

Steak in Mustard Marinade

4 sirloin steaks, 125g (4oz) each

1 tblspn hot English mustard

1 tblspn honey

1 clove garlic, crushed

½ cup beer

1 Remove fat from steaks. Marinate steaks in mixture of remaining ingredients 30 minutes. Drain steak, reserve marinade.

2 Barbecue steaks until well browned. Brush steaks with marinade while cooking.

Serves 4

Steak in Mustard Marinade

Pork in Prune and Almond Sauce

4 pork loin medallions, 125g (4oz) each, all visible fat removed

1 tblspn olive oil

1 onion, finely chopped

1 clove garlic, crushed

1 tspn French mustard

2 tspn paprika

1 tblspn chopped prunes

1 tblspn port

2 tspn cornflour

¾ cup skim milk

1 tblspn slivered almonds

1 spring onion (scallion), green part only, finely sliced

1 Heat oil in pan, brown pork on both sides, remove from pan.

2 Add onion and garlic to pan, cook for 5 minutes. Add mustard, paprika, prunes and port, cook for 2 minutes.

3 Add combined cornflour and skim milk, cook until mixture boils and thickens.

4 Return pork to pan, simmer slowly for 10 minutes or until pork is tender.

5 Meanwhile toast almonds on oven tray in moderate oven for 5 minutes. Serve pork sprinkled with almonds and spring onions.

Serves 4

Veal Marsala

375g (¾lb) veal schnitzel

1 tblspn olive oil

1 clove garlic, crushed

2 tblspn marsala

1 tblspn lemon juice

1 tblspn chopped parsley

1 Heat oil in pan, cook veal for 3 minutes each side or until just cooked. Remove veal to heated dish.

2 Add garlic, marsala and lemon juice to pan. Stir well to combine with pan juices.

3 Return veal to pan, cook until heated through. Sprinkle with parsley before serving.

Serves 4

Stir-fry Chicken with Cashews

375g (¾lb) chicken breast fillets, cut into strips

1 tblspn olive oil

1 red onion, cut into petals

1 carrot, diagonally sliced

1 clove garlic, crushed

1 tspn grated ginger

2 tspn olive oil, extra

250g (½lb) broccoli, cut into flowerets

2 tblspn unsalted cashew nuts

½ cup degreased chicken stock

3 spring onions (scallions), diagonally sliced

2 tspn cornflour

2 tspn shoyu or tamari (see note)

1 tblspn sherry

¼ tspn sesame oil

1 Heat oil in pan, cook onion and carrot 5 minutes. Add garlic and ginger, cook 1 minute. Remove from pan.

2 Cook chicken in batches until lightly browned. Remove from pan.

3 Heat extra oil in pan, cook broccoli and cashew nuts until cashews are lightly browned.

4 Return vegetables and chicken to pan with stock, shallots and combined cornflour, shoyu, sherry and sesame oil. Cook until mixture boils and thickens. Serve with rice.

Serves 4

Note: Shoyu and tamari are available at healthfood shops.

Stir-fry Chicken with Cashews

Sate Lamb with Peanut Sauce

500g (1lb) lean lamb, cubed

2 tspn soy sauce

1 tspn honey

½ tspn chilli powder

2 tspn cumin

1 tspn curry powder

2 tblspn olive oil

PEANUT SAUCE:

1 tblspn oil

1 onion, finely chopped

1 clove garlic, crushed

¼ tspn chilli powder

1 tspn curry powder

1 tspn grated ginger

½ cup crunchy peanut butter

¼ cup vinegar

2 tblspn sugar

2 tblspn sweet fruit chutney

1 Place lamb in dish. Add combined remaining ingredients, mix well. Refrigerate overnight.

2 Thread lamb onto bamboo skewers. Grill on both sides until golden and just cooked. Serve with Peanut Sauce.

3 To make peanut sauce: Heat oil in pan, cook onion for 5 minutes, stirring occasionally. Add remaining ingredients, bring to boil, simmer for 15 minutes, stirring occasionally.

Serves 4

Chicken with Ginger and Peanuts

1 tblspn olive oil

500g (1lb) chicken breasts, cut into 2.5cm (1in) cubes

⅓ cup dry white wine

1 tspn grated ginger

1 clove garlic, crushed

1 cup chicken stock

⅓ cup crunchy peanut butter

2 spring onions (scallions), julienned

1 red chilli, sliced

1 Marinate chicken in mixture of wine, ginger and garlic for 30 minutes, drain, reserve marinade.

2 Heat oil in pan, cook chicken until almost cooked, add marinade and combined stock and peanut butter. Bring to boil, reduce heat, simmer 5 minutes. Add spring onions and chilli, cook 1 minute before serving.

Serves 4

Devilled Chicken Fillets

4 chicken breast fillets, 125g (4oz) each

½ cup sweet fruit chutney

1 tspn curry powder

2 tspn olive oil

1 tblspn low salt soy sauce

1 tspn dry mustard

1 Arrange chicken fillets in lightly oiled shallow ovenproof dish.

2 Combine remaining ingredients, pour over chicken. Turn chicken to coat all over.

3 Bake in moderate oven for 12 minutes or until just cooked through.

Serves 4

Beef in Red Wine

500g (1lb) lean chuck steak, cubed

plain flour

1 tblspn olive oil

1 onion, chopped

1 clove garlic, crushed

1 tblspn brandy

125g (4oz) mushrooms

1 tblspn olive oil, extra

1 cup degreased beef stock

1 cup dry red wine

400g (13oz) can peeled tomatoes, undrained

¼ cup tomato paste

2 tblspn chopped parsley

1 Heat oil in pan, cook onion for 5 minutes, add garlic, brandy and mushrooms, cook for 3 minutes. Place onion mixture in casserole dish.

2 Heat extra oil in pan. Dust beef cubes in flour. Cook in batches until browned all over. Add beef stock, red wine, tomatoes and tomato paste. Bring to boil, pour into casserole dish, mix well.

3 Bake, covered, in moderately slow oven for 1½ hours. Add parsley. Serve with rice and salad.

Serves 4

Chicken with Ginger and Peanuts

PERFECT PARTNERS

These tasty side dishes are a wonderful alternative to plain vegetables and provide excellent amounts of dietary fibre, vitamins and minerals.

Marinated Mushroom and Pimento Salad

2 tblspn lemon juice

2 tblspn red wine vinegar

2 tblspn white wine vinegar

2 cloves garlic, crushed

1 tblspn chopped fresh basil

1 tblspn chopped fresh parsley

2 tblspn safflower oil

8 pimentos, sliced into strips

1 cup mushrooms, sliced

1 In a medium bowl, mix together lemon juice, red vinegar, white vinegar, garlic, basil, parsley and oil, until well combined.

2 Stir in the pimentos and mushrooms, cover and chill for 3 hours. Serve chilled as a side dish.

Serves 4

Zucchini (Courgette) and Tomato with Sesame Seeds

2 tblspn sesame seeds

2 cloves garlic, finely chopped

2 tspn olive oil

6 zucchini (courgette), sliced

6 spring onions (scallions), chopped

2 tomatoes, cut into 8 wedges each

⅓ cup chopped fresh basil

1 Place sesame seeds on a baking tray in a 180°C (350°F) oven. Bake about 10 minutes, or until seeds are golden. Cool. Set aside.

2 In a frying pan saute garlic in oil until golden. Add zucchini and spring onions, saute about 5 minutes, until zucchini is nearly tender but still crisp.

3 Add tomatoes and basil. Cook until heated through, stirring gently.

4 Serve on a heated platter, sprinkled with toasted sesame seeds, 1 cup per person.

Serves 4

Marinated Mushrooms and Pimento Salad

Potato Bullets

Don't let the name put you off this delicious crispy potato dish; it doesn't refer to the texture, rather the shape.

3 potatoes, peeled, cut into eights

⅓ onion

3 egg whites

pepper·

½ tspn baking powder

mild paprika

1 Place potatoes and onion in a processor. Process until finely chopped, stopping once to scrape sides.

2 Add egg whites, freshly ground pepper and baking powder. Process just long enough to combine.

3 Place ⅓ cup of the mixture in each of eight non-stick muffin cups. Sprinkle with paprika.

4 Bake in a 200°C (400°F) oven for 20 minutes, lower heat to 180°C (350°F), bake a further 20 minutes, or until golden.

5 Turn potato bullets out onto a heated platter, serve hot, 1 bullet per person.

Serves 8

French Bean and Chickpea Salad

250g (½lb) French beans, topped and tailed

1 cup cooked chickpeas

½ cucumber, seeded, sliced

½ red capsicum (pepper), seeded, cut into thin strips

½ Spanish onion, cut into half rings

⅓ cup vinaigrette (see page 24)

¼ cup chopped fresh basil

1 small mignonette lettuce

4 cherry tomatoes, halved

Beetroot Slices with Yoghurt

1 Plunge beans into boiling water, return to a boil, cook 2 minutes, drain. Pat dry. Cool.

2 In a bowl combine cooled beans, chickpeas, cucumber, capsicum, onion and basil. Add vinaigrette, toss well, cover. Refrigerate at least 2 hours.

3 Line a platter with mignonette leaves, arrange salad on top. Scatter with tomato. Serve cold, ¾ cup per person.

Serves 4

Beetroot Slices with Yoghurt

8 fresh baby beets

16 radicchio leaves

bunch fresh parsley

¾ cup natural non fat yoghurt

1 Clean beets, cut off tops and tails. Place in a casserole dish and bake, covered, for 1 hour in a moderate oven, or until tender. Slip skins off, and chill.

2 Arrange lettuce on serving plate, arrange parsley. Slice beets and place on top of parsley.

3 Pour yoghurt over beetroot and serve immediately.

Serves 4

Corn and Zucchini (Courgette) Casserole

Corn and Zucchini (Courgette) Casserole

2½ cups cooked corn kernels, drained

4 zucchini (courgette), cut into slices

3 ripe tomatoes, chopped

½ cup tomato puree

1 large onion, peeled and chopped

1 red capsicum (pepper), seeded and chopped

4 cups degreased chicken stock

1 In a large deep frying pan add corn, zucchini, tomatoes, tomato puree, onion and capsicum, cook for 15 minutes.

2 Add the stock and bring to the boil, reduce heat, simmer for 25 minutes. Serve hot.

Serves 6

Rosemary Crispy Potatoes

750g (1½lb) potatoes

1 bunch spring onions (scallions), chopped

1 tblspn chopped fresh rosemary

salt

pepper

1 tspn safflower oil

⅓ cup degreased chicken stock

rosemary sprigs for garnish

1 Boil potatoes in skin until tender. When cool enough to handle, peel, cut into 2cm (¾in) cubes.

2 In a bowl combine potatoes with spring onions and rosemary. Season very lightly with salt and generously with freshly ground black pepper. Toss well.

3 Brush a baking dish with oil, spoon potato mixture into dish. Pour over chicken stock.

4 Bake on a high shelf in a 200°C (400°F) oven for about 50 minutes. Stir every 15 minutes to allow potatoes to brown evenly. Serve hot, 1 cup per person.

Serves 4

Broccoli Salad with Hazelnuts

2 cups broccoli flowerets

45g (1½oz) sliced hazelnuts

DRESSING:

¼ cup non fat yoghurt

1 tblspn lemon juice

1 small clove garlic, crushed

2 tblspn finely chopped onion

1 tblspn tomato ketchup

1/8 tspn tabasco sauce

1 Steam broccoli flowerets until almost tender, but still crisp. Cool.

2 In a small bowl combine dressing ingredients, mix well. Cover, refrigerate at least 1 hour.

3 Spread hazelnuts on an oven tray, bake in a 180°C (350°F) oven until light brown. Cool.

4 Place broccoli in a salad bowl, toss with chilled dressing. Sprinkle with toasted hazelnuts. Serve ½ cup per person.

Serves 4

Mediterranean Eggplant (Aubergine)

1 large eggplant (aubergine)

1 tspn salt

1 tblspn olive oil

½ cup black olives, stoned

1 tspn capers, drained

½ tspn oregano

¼ cup freshly squeezed lemon juice

1 Cut eggplant into 2cm (¾in) pieces. Place in a colander, sprinkle with salt. Place a plate with a heavy weight on top of eggplant to draw out bitter juices. Leave 1 hour.

2 Rinse under cold running water. Squeeze pieces to release juices.

3 Steam eggplant until tender.

4 In a frying pan combine oil, eggplant, olives, capers, oregano and lemon juice. Cook over medium low heat until heated through and flavours mingle.

Serves 6

Basil, Orange and Peach Salad

1 bunch fresh basil

6 navel oranges, peeled and segmented

3 orange peaches, peeled and sliced

1 red onion, peeled and sliced

2 tblspn red wine vinegar

1 garlic clove, crushed

2 tblspn unsweetened apple juice

2 tblspn safflower oil

1 Wash and dry basil leaves, arrange on a serving plate.

2 In a small bowl combine orange segments, peach slices and onion.

3 Mix together vinegar, garlic, apple juice and oil until well combined and pour over oranges, peaches and onion.

4 Toss well, and arrange on top of bed of basil. Serve immediately.

Serves 6

Basil, Orange and Peach Salad

Coleslaw with Apples and Sultanas

375g (¾lb) cabbage, shredded

1 stalk celery, thinly sliced

2 carrots, cut into matchsticks

1 Granny Smith apple, unpeeled, cored, quartered, cut into thin slices

2 tblspn sultanas

⅓ cup Creamy Dressing (see page 22)

⅓ cup chopped parsley

1 Combine cabbage, celery and carrots in a bowl. Add apple and sultanas.

2 Add dressing, toss well. Sprinkle with parsley. Cover, refrigerate at least 2 hours. Serve cold, ¾ cup per person.

Serves 4

Spinach, Mushroom and Beansprout Salad

This salad is pretty, high in fibre, and low in kilojoules

½ bunch spinach, about 6 leaves

90g (3oz) button mushrooms

250g (½lb) beansprouts, rinsed, drained

½ red capsicum (pepper), seeded, cut into thin strips

⅓ cup vinaigrette (see page 24)

1 thinly sliced Spanish onion

1 Rinse spinach in several changes of cold water. Remove stems, tear into bite-size pieces. Pat dry with paper towels.

2 Combine spinach in a salad bowl with mushrooms, beansprouts and capsicum. Cover, refrigerate at least 1 hour.

3 Toss salad with vinaigrette, add onion rings, serve cold.

Serves 4

Waldorf Salad with Pecans

2 Granny Smith apples

2 red Delicious apples

2 tblspn lemon juice

1½ cups sliced celery

½ cup pecan halves, roasted

DRESSING:

200g (6½oz) carton low fat plain yoghurt

1 tspn honey

pinch each cinnamon and nutmeg

1 Core and quarter apples, slice thinly, dip in lemon juice.

2 Combine with celery in bowl. Add pecans, toss lightly.

4 Combine ingredients for dressing, mix well. Pour over salad, toss well.

Serves 4

Spinach and Sesame Seed Salad

1 tblspn sesame seeds

1 tblspn tahini

1 tspn sesame oil

1½ tblspn shoyu (see note)

1 tblspn rice vinegar

2 tblspn olive oil

1 tspn grated ginger

500g (1lb) spinach, stalks removed, washed and dried

125g (4oz) small mushrooms, sliced

125g (4oz) cherry tomatoes, halved

1 Toast sesame seeds on oven tray in moderate oven 10 minutes. Set aside.

2 Combine tahini, sesame oil, shoyu, rice vinegar, oil and ginger in a jar, shake well.

3 Tear spinach into pieces and place in salad bowl with mushrooms and tomatoes. Pour dressing over and toss well.

4 Sprinkle with sesame seeds before serving.

Serves 4

Note: Shoyu is a type of soy sauce available from healthfood shops.

Spinach and Sesame Seed Salad

Broccoli with Red Capsicum (Pepper) Puree

500g (1lb) broccoli, cut into flowerets

1 tblspn olive oil

1 clove garlic, crushed

2 red capsicums (pepper), seeded and chopped

½ cup degreased chicken stock

1 tblspn white wine vinegar

1 tspn chopped tarragon

1 tspn horseradish cream

1 Boil, steam or microwave broccoli until just tender, keep warm.

2 Heat oil in pan, add garlic and capsicum, cook 2 minutes. Pour in stock, vinegar, tarragon and horseradish, bring to the boil, reduce heat, simmer 5 minutes or until capsicum is tender.

3 Blend or process mixture until smooth. Place broccoli in serving dish, pour sieved red capsicum puree over top.

Serves 4

Broccoli with Red Capsicum Sauce

Green and Red Salad

1 bunch asparagus, cut into 2.5cm (1in) lengths

1 red capsicum (pepper), cut into strips

4 spring onions (scallions), cut into 2.5cm (1in) lengths

2 Lebanese cucumbers, cut into strips

1 butter lettuce, washed

2 tblspn balsamic vinegar

2 tblspn olive oil

1 clove garlic, crushed

1 Cook asparagus in boiling water 1 minute, drain. Run under cold water until cold.

2 Combine asparagus, red capsicum, spring onions and Lebanese cucumbers in bowl.

3 Combine vinegar, oil and garlic in jar, shake well, pour over asparagus mixture. Toss well. Serve salad in cups of butter lettuce leaves.

Serves 4

Potato Salad with Mango Dressing

12-14 baby new potatoes

1 ripe mango, chopped

⅓ cup low fat plain yoghurt

1 tblspn lime juice

1 tblspn oil

1 small red onion chopped

1 Boil potatoes in boiling water 8 minutes or until just tender. Drain. Cool under cold running water. When cold cut in half.

2 Blend or process mango with yoghurt, lime juice and oil until smooth.

3 Combine potatoes in bowl with mango dressing and red onion.

Serves 4

Vegetable Stir-fry

1 tblspn olive oil

1 clove garlic, crushed

1 tspn grated ginger

½ tspn sesame oil

1 bunch asparagus, cut into diagonal lengths

125g (4oz) beans, cut into diagonal lengths

125g (4oz) snowpeas, cut into diagonal lengths

1 carrot, cut into diagonal slices

1 red capsicum (pepper), cut into diamonds

1 Heat oil in pan, add garlic, ginger and sesame oil, cook 30 seconds.

2 Add vegetables, stir-fry 3 minutes or until just tender.

Serves 4

Above: Julienne Salad

Below: Vegetable Stir-fry

Julienne Salad

125g (4oz) carrots, julienned

2 zucchini (courgette), julienned

1 red capsicum (pepper), julienned

1 green capsicum (pepper), julienned

1 stick celery, julienned

4 spring onions (scallions), julienned

1 tblspn tarragon vinegar

2 tblspn walnut oil

1 clove garlic, crushed

1 Place julienned (cut into thin strips) vegetables into salad bowl.

2 Combine vinegar, oil and garlic in a jar, shake well, pour over salad and toss well.

3 Refrigerate, covered, for 3 hours.

Serves 4

103

BETTER BAKING

Cakes and loaves needn't be excluded from a healthy diet. These tempting treats not only taste good, they are good for you.

Country Apple Flan

PASTRY:

1½ cups plain flour

¼ tspn salt

¾ tspn dry yeast

¾ cup warm water

FILLING:

2 tblspn honey

3 green apples, cored, peeled and thinly sliced

2 tspn cinnamon sugar

2 tblspn brown sugar

1 Combine flour and salt in a large bowl. In a separate small bowl mix the yeast with the warm water and let stand until yeast has dissolved, approximately 4 minutes.

2 Make a well in the centre of flour mixture, pour in yeast mixture gradually while stirring in flour.

3 Knead dough until smooth and elastic, approximately 10 minutes. Place dough in a large bowl, cover with a tea towel and leave for 1 hour, in a warm place, to double in size.

4 Punch down dough, and leave to rise again for 30 minutes.

5 Roll out dough to fit a 23cm (9in) flan dish and bake blind for 15 minutes.

6 Brush honey over pastry, arrange apple slices on top and sprinkle with combined cinnamon sugar and brown sugar. Bake in a moderate oven for 30 minutes.

Serves 12

Peanut Butter Biscuits

1 cup plain flour

½ tspn baking soda

½ cup margarine

½ cup peanut butter

½ cup brown sugar

½ cup plain sugar

2 egg whites

½ tspn vanilla essence

1 Sift flour and baking soda into a bowl. Set aside.

2 In a processor combine margarine and peanut butter. Process until creamy. Add sugars, egg whites and vanilla essence. Process until well combined.

3 Add flour, process until you have a smooth dough.

4 Place teaspoons of dough onto a baking sheet, flatten with a floured fork. Bake in a 180°C (350°F) oven until golden, about 10 minutes.

5 Cool on baking sheet for 2 minutes. Remove to wire rack to cool completely, store in an airtight container.

Makes about 60

Country Apple Flan

Blueberry Pecan Loaf

1 cup wholemeal flour

1 cup plain flour

1 cup sugar

1½ tspn baking powder

1 tspn salt

½ tspn baking soda

¼ cup margarine

½ cup freshly squeezed orange juice

¼ cup freshly squeezed lemon juice

1 tblspn grated lemon rind

2 egg whites

1 cup blueberries

1 cup chopped pecan nuts

1 Sift flours, sugar, baking powder, salt and baking soda into a processor. Add margarine, process until mixture resembles coarse crumbs.

2 Combine juices, rind and egg whites in a separate bowl, mix well. Add to processor, process just long enough to moisten. Add blueberries and nuts, process just long enough to combine.

3 Spoon into a greased loaf pan, bake in a 180°C (350°F) oven until tester comes out clean, about 1 hour. Cool in pan on a rack. Turn out, cut into 1cm (½in) slices.

Gives about 18 slices

Pistachio Oat Bran Biscuits

⅓ cup margarine

⅔ cup sugar

1 tspn vanilla essence

½ tspn baking soda

½ tspn cream of tartar

1 cup plain flour

½ cup oat bran

⅓ cup buttermilk

¼ cup chopped pistachio nuts

1 Combine margarine and sugar in a bowl, beat until creamy. Add vanilla, baking soda and cream of tartar. Mix in well.

2 Combine flour and oat bran, fold in alternately with buttermilk in three batches, mixing well after each addition. Fold in pistachios.

3 Place teaspoons of the mixture on a lightly greased baking sheet. Bake in a 200°C (400°F) oven until golden, about 10 minutes.

4 Remove baking sheet from oven, cool biscuits on sheet for 2 minutes. Removed biscuits to wire rack to cool completely. Store in an airtight container.

Makes about 30 biscuits

Apricot Oat Slices

150g (5oz) margarine

1¼ cups brown sugar

1¾ cups plain flour

½ tspn bicarbonate of soda

1½ cups rolled oats

¾ cup apricot jam

1 Beat together margarine and sugar with electric mixer until creamy.

2 Beat in flour and bicarbonate until well combined, stir in oats.

3 Press half the mixture into a greaseproof paper lined 19cm x 29cm (7½ x 11½in) lamington tin.

4 Spread jam over the top and sprinkle with the remaining oat mixture.

5 Bake in a moderate oven for 30 minutes. Cool in tin, cut into triangles.

Makes 24

*Pecan Crispies (top);
Apricot Oat Slices (right)*

Pecan Crispies

3 egg whites

pinch salt

1 tspn vanilla essence

¾ cup castor sugar

2 cups pecan nuts, chopped

1 Beat egg whites in a large bowl with an electric mixer until soft peaks form.

2 Add salt, vanilla and sugar, beat for a further 1 minute, fold in nuts.

3 Drop teaspoonfuls of mixture onto a greaseproof paper lined baking tray.

4 Bake in moderate oven for 2-3 minutes, turn off oven and leave biscuits in oven for 60 minutes.

5 Use a spatula to ease biscuits off paper, store in an airtight container.

Makes about 6 dozen

Chocolate Cake

1¾ cups plain flour

1 tblspn baking powder

1 tspn salt

½ cup cocoa powder

1¼ cups sugar

1 cup skim milk

½ cup safflower oil

1 tspn vanilla essence

4 egg whites

1 Sift combined flour, baking powder, salt, cocoa powder and 1 cup of the sugar into a bowl. Add milk, oil and vanilla essence, mix well with an electric mixer, scraping down sides of bowl.

2 Beat egg whites until soft peaks form. Slowly add remaining sugar. Keep beating until stiff peaks form.

3 Fold whites into batter. Spoon into a greased and lightly floured loaf pan. Bake in 180°C (350°F) oven for about 40 minutes, or until tester comes out clean.

4 Remove from oven, stand in pan for 5 minutes, turn out, cool on a wire rack. Serve sliced.

Gives about 24 slices

Mocha Hazelnut Meringues

1 cup chopped hazelnuts

4 egg whites

1 tspn vanilla essence

1/8 tspn cream of tartar

½ cup icing sugar, sifted

1½ tblspn unsweetened cocoa powder

1 tblspn instant coffee, dissolved in 2 tspn boiling water

1 Spread hazelnuts on a baking tray. Toast in a 180°C (350°F) oven until golden, about 10-15 minutes. Cool. Set aside.

2 Beat egg whites until soft peaks form. Add vanilla and cream of tartar, continue beating, adding sugar and cocoa powder little by little, until stiff peaks form. Add coffee, beat well to incorporate.

3 Mix in hazelnuts. Drop heaped teaspoons of the mixture onto a baking sheet lined with greased greaseproof paper. Bake in a 110°C (225°F) oven for 1 hour. Turn off heat, leave meringues in oven for 5 minutes. Remove from oven, cool on a wire rack. Store in an airtight container.

Makes about 40

One egg yolk contains about 285mg cholesterol, which is a lot, considering 300mg per day is the absolute limit. If your blood cholesterol levels are too high, it would be more appropriate to keep your daily cholesterol intake down to 100mg.

Banana Cake

500g (1lb) ripe bananas, mashed (about 3 large)

45g (1½oz) chopped walnuts

¾ cup sunflower oil

105g (3½oz) sultanas

75g (2½oz) rolled oats

155g (5oz) whole wheat flour

2 tspn baking powder

¼ cup sugar

1 Mix all ingredients together in bowl. Spread into a greased and paper-lined loaf tin.

2 Bake in moderate oven 1 hour or until a skewer inserted into centre comes out clean.

3 Cool 10 minutes before turning onto wire rack to cool completely.

Makes 1 cake

Wholemeal Damper

1 cup wholemeal self-raising flour

1 cup white self-raising flour

1⅓ cups skim milk

1 tspn dry mustard

1 tblspn sesame seeds

1 Sift flours into bowl, return husks from sifter to bowl. Stir in enough skim milk to give a sticky dough. Knead on lightly floured surface until smooth, shape into a round.

2 Place dough onto lightly greased oven tray, press out with fingers to about 3cm (1¼in) thick. Using a sharp knife mark into wedges, cut wedges into dough about 1cm (½in) deep.

3 Sprinkle dough with combined mustard and sesame seeds. Bake in hot oven for 30 minutes, or until golden brown and damper sounds hollow when tapped with fingers.

Makes 1 damper

Banana Cake

Date Cake

¾ cup chopped dates

½ cup apple juice

½ cup low fat plain yoghurt

1 egg white

2 cups wholemeal self-raising flour

½ tspn mixed spice

¼ cup skim milk

1 Place dates and apple juice in pan, bring to boil, remove from heat, cool.

2 Combine yoghurt, egg white and skim milk, mix well. Add combined flour and mixed spice. Fold date mixture into flour mixture.

3 Pour into greased and paper lined loaf tin. Bake in moderate oven 30 minutes or until skewer inserted in centre comes out clean. Cool 10 minutes before turning onto wire rack to cool.

Makes 1 cake

Christmas Cake

1½ cups sultanas

1½ cups currants

1 cup raisins, chopped

1 cup dates, chopped

2 tblspn chopped almonds

2 tblspn chopped walnuts

¼ cup brandy

1 cup apple juice

1½ cups wholemeal self-raising flour

⅓ cup unprocessed bran

1 apple, grated

3 egg whites

1 tspn nutmeg

1 tspn cinnamon

½ cup skim milk

1 Place fruit and nuts in bowl with brandy and apple juice, cover and stand overnight.

2 Sift flour and spices into a bowl, return husks to bowl. Add to fruit and nut mixture with bran, apple, egg whites and skim milk.

3 Prepare a deep 20cm (8in) round cake tin by lining base and sides with three thicknesses of greaseproof paper. Bring lining paper 5cm (2in) above edge of tin. Spread mixture evenly into tin, decorate top with almonds if desired.

4 Bake in slow oven for 2 hours or until a skewer inserted in centre comes out clean.

5 Cover cake with foil and wrap whole cake in a tea-towel, stand overnight. Remove from tin when cold.

Makes 1 cake

Apple And Apricot Loaf

250g (½lb) dried apricots, chopped

125g (4oz) dried apples, chopped

1¼ cup orange juice

1 cup grated apple

½ cup grated carrot

1 tblspn cocoa

1 tspn mixed spice

2 egg whites, lightly beaten

1½ cup wholemeal self-raising flour

1 tspn baking powder

1 Combine dried fruits with orange juice in a saucepan, bring to a boil, remove from heat, cool to room temperature.

2 Stir in remaining ingredients, mix well.

3 Spoon into a greased and lined loaf pan and bake in moderate oven for 1 hour or until cooked through. Turn onto wire rack to cool.

Makes 1 loaf

Apple and Apricot Loaf

Oatmeal Biscuits

2 ripe bananas, mashed

½ cup brown sugar

3 tspn vanilla essence

3 egg whites

1 cup plain flour

1 cup self-raising flour

1½ cups 1-minute oats

½ tspn bicarbonate of soda

½ cup evaporated skim milk

½ cup chopped hazelnuts

1 Combine bananas in bowl with sugar, vanilla and egg whites.

2 Combine flours, oats and bicarbonate of soda in another bowl. Alternately add the flour mixture and milk to banana mixture. Add hazelnuts.

3 Place teaspoons of mixture onto lightly greased oven tray. Bake in moderate oven 10 minutes or until slightly browned on edges. Cool on wire rack.

Makes about 40

Oat Bran Muffins

1¼ cups oat bran

1 cup self-raising flour

1½ cups evaporated skim milk

2 egg whites, lightly beaten

¼ cup honey

3 tblspn safflower oil

1 Mix oat bran and flour in large bowl.

2 Blend or process milk, egg whites, honey and oil until smooth, add to flour mixture. Stir until just mixed.

3 Line a muffin tin with paper cups and fill with mixture.

4 Bake in moderately hot oven 15 minutes or until skewer inserted in centre comes out clean.

Makes 12

Wholemeal Date Scones

1 cup unprocessed bran

1 cup wholemeal self-raising flour

1 cup white self-raising flour

60g (2oz) polyunsaturated margarine

125g (4oz) dates, finely chopped

1 cup skim milk

1 Sift flours into bowl, return husks from sifter to bowl, mix in bran. Rub in margarine, add dates.

2 Make well in centre of dry ingredients, stir in enough milk to give a soft, sticky dough.

3 Turn dough onto lightly floured surface and knead lightly until smooth. Press dough out to 1cm (½in) thickness, cut into rounds with 5cm (2in) cutter.

4 Place scones into greased slab tin, bake in moderately hot oven 15 minutes or until golden brown.

Makes about 15

Carrot Cake

90g (3oz) polyunsaturated margarine

½ cup brown sugar

2 egg whites

1 cup grated carrot

2 ripe bananas, mashed

1½ cups plain flour

1 tspn bicarbonate of soda

½ tspn cinnamon

¼ cup chopped walnuts

¼ cup sultanas

1 Cream margarine and sugar until just combined, add egg whites and beat well. Stir in carrot and bananas.

2 Add combined sifted flour, bicarbonate of soda, cinnamon walnuts and sultanas. Mix well. Pour into a greased and paper lined loaf tin.

3 Bake in moderate oven 1 hour or until a skewer inserted in the centre comes out clean.

4 Stand 5 minutes. Turn onto wire rack to cool.

Makes 1 cake

Wholemeal Bran Bread

500g (1lb) wholemeal plain flour

½ cup plain white flour

½ cup gluten flour

¼ cup skim milk powder

1 tspn salt

1 cup unprocessed bran

½ tspn sugar

15g (½oz) compressed yeast

1½ cups warm water, approximately

1 Sift flours into large bowl, return husks from sifter to bowl, add milk powder and salt, mix in bran.

2 Make well in centre, add sugar, crumbled yeast and ¼ cup of the water. Cover bowl with plastic food wrap, stand in warm place for 15 minutes, or until the mixture in the centre has become foamy.

3 Gradually work in enough of the remaining water to give a firm pliable dough. Knead dough on a floured surface 5 minutes or until smooth and elastic. Place in greased bowl, cover with plastic wrap; stand in warm place 1 hour or until dough has doubled in bulk.

4 Turn dough onto floured surface, knead until smooth. Knead into loaf shape, place into greased bread tin. Stand uncovered in warm place 30 minutes or until dough is well risen. Bake in moderately hot oven 40 minutes.

5 Remove loaf from tin, place on side on oven rack, bake further 10 minutes, turn loaf, bake further 10 minutes, cool on wire rack.

Makes 1 loaf

Wholemeal Date Scones

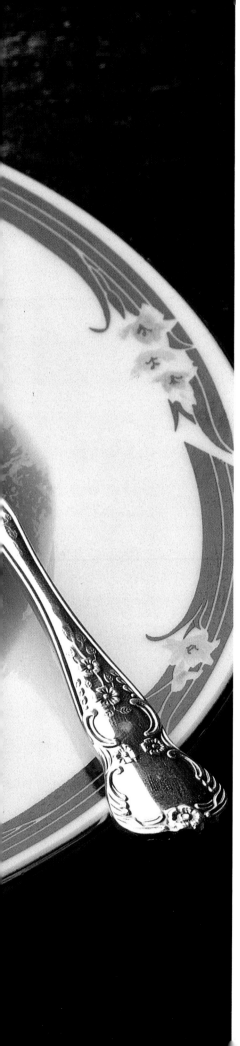

DELICIOUS DESSERTS

These wonderful desserts will provide a spectacular finale to any meal without adding cholesterol to your diet.

Mixed Berry Meringues with Apricot Coulis

3 egg whites, at room temperature

⅓ cup castor sugar

1 tspn vanilla essence

½ cup raspberries

½ cup blueberries

3 tblspn Grand Marnier

1 cup tinned apricot halves, drained

¼ cup apricot nectar

1 Beat egg whites with electric mixer until light and fluffy. Slowly add sugar while motor is running.

2 Add vanilla and beat for a further 10 minutes until mixture is thick and glossy.

3 Place mixture into a piping bag and pipe nests approximately 6cm (2½in) in diameter onto a greased paper-lined baking tray.

4 Bake in a moderately low oven for 20 minutes, reduce heat to 120°C (250°F) and bake for a further 25 minutes.

5 In a small bowl combine raspberries, blueberries and Grand Marnier and place berries in the centre of meringue nests.

6 In a food processor or blender, process apricot halves with apricot nectar until smooth.

7 Spoon 2 tablespoons of apricot coulis onto each serving plate, place meringue nest in centre of coulis, decorate with fresh sprig of mint if desired.

Serves 4-6

Walnut Apple Strudel

4 Jonathan apples, peeled, cored, sliced

¼ cup chopped walnuts

1 tblspn low fat plain yoghurt

1½ tblspn sugar

2 tspn ground cinnamon

4 sheets filo pastry

2 tblspn safflower oil

1 egg white

1 Combine apple, walnuts, yoghurt, sugar and cinnamon in a bowl. Mix well. Chill in refrigerator for 20 minutes.

2 Place a sheet of filo pastry on bench, brush lightly with oil, repeat layering with remaining pastry, brushing every sheet with oil.

3 Place filling along one edge of long side, leaving a 5cm (2in) border on sides and front. Fold sides in and roll up. Brush all over with beaten egg white.

4 Place on a lightly greased oven tray, bake in a 180°C (350°F) oven until golden, about 50 minutes. Serve warm or at room temperature, 2.5cm (1in) slices per person.

Serves 6

Mixed Berry Meringues with Apricot Coulis

Flambe Cherries with Vanilla Ice

2 cups low fat vanilla yoghurt

500g (1lb) cherries, stoned (see note)

⅓ cup brown sugar

⅓ cup cherry brandy

2 tblspn Kirsch

1 Place yoghurt in an ice-cream machine, freeze according to manufacturer's instructions.

2 Heat cherries and sugar in a frying pan over medium heat.

3 Add cherry brandy and Kirsch, ignite, shake pan over heat until flames die down. Simmer 4 minutes.

4 Spoon onto dessert plates, serve with frozen yoghurt.

Note: If fresh cherries are not available, substitute with drained, canned black cherries.

Serves 4

Strawberry Mousse

2½ cups strawberries, hulled

¼ cup orange juice

1 tblspn gelatine

1 tblspn cherry brandy

3 egg whites

3 tblspn sugar

1 Place strawberries in a food processor, puree.

2 Combine orange juice and gelatine, add to strawberries in processor, process just long enough to blend. Pour into a saucepan.

3 Place over low heat, stirring constantly, until gelatine is dissolved. Add cherry brandy. Pour into a bowl, cover, refrigerate until mixture starts to set.

4 Beat egg whites until foamy. Add sugar little by little, beat until stiff. Fold into strawberry mixture. Pour into a 4-cup mould, a souffle dish is fine. Chill until set, about 4 hours or overnight.

Serves 6

Pear and Peach Champagne Sorbet

Pear and Peach Champagne Sorbet

2 cups chopped tinned pears

2 cups chopped tinned peaches

½ cup sugar

⅔ cup champagne

1 In a food processor or blender process fruit until smooth.

2 Combine sugar and champagne in a large saucepan and simmer gently until sugar has dissolved.

3 Stir in the pureed fruit, pour mixture into a freezeproof container, cover and place in freezer.

4 Remove sorbet from freezer every 30 minutes for 3 hours and stir, breaking up crystals.

5 Freeze for another 2 hours or until firm. Decorate with strips of lime rind if desired.

Serves 6

Glazed Strawberry Flan

PASTRY:

1½ cups plain flour

¼ tspn salt

⅓ cup safflower oil

3 tblspn iced water

FILLING:

2 punnets strawberries, stems removed

¾ cup sugar

2 tblspn cornflour

2 tblspn white corn syrup

1 cup water

2 tblspn strawberry jelly crystals

Glazed Strawberry Flan

1 Mix together flour and salt. Whisk the oil and water together and pour into flour mixture. Stir with a metal spoon, form into a ball and knead gently for 30 seconds.

2 Roll pastry out between 2 sheets of greaseproof paper to fit a 23cm (9in) flan tin and bake blind in moderately hot oven for 15 minutes.

3 In a medium saucepan, combine sugar, cornflour, corn syrup and water over medium heat. Gently bring to boil and cook for 2 minutes. Stir in jelly crystals until dissolved; cool slightly.

4 Arrange strawberries decoratively over pastry flan and pour jelly mixture evenly over strawberries. Chill until set.

Serves 8

Lime Rice Pudding

½ cup rice
1½ cups water
⅓ cup raisins
1/8 tspn ground nutmeg
1 cup skim milk
¼ cup sugar
1 tspn grated lime rind
1 tspn lime juice
½ tspn vanilla essence

1 Combine rice, water, raisins and nutmeg in the top of a double boiler. Mix well, cover, cook over boiling water for 20 minutes.

2 Add milk, mix well. Cook without lid until milk has been absorbed, about 10 minutes. Stir in sugar, cool.

3 Add lime rind, juice and vanilla mix thoroughly. Place into a serving dish, cover, refrigerate at least 2 hours. Serve chilled.

Serves 6

Bananas Flamed with Rum

4 peeled bananas
1 tblspn lemon juice
1 tblspn brown sugar
2 tblspn rum

1 Place bananas in a lightly greased baking dish. Sprinkle with lemon juice and brown sugar.

2 Bake in a 200°C (400°F) oven until golden brown, about 20 minutes. Remove from oven.

3 Pour over rum, ignite. When flames have died down, serve.

Serves 4

Peach Meringue Pie

¾ cup egg white, at room temperature

¼ tspn cream of tartar

1½ tspn vanilla essence

¾ cup pureed ripe banana

1 cup canned evaporated skim milk

4 cups sliced peaches

1 tspn almond essence

2 tblspn apricot liqueur

1 Beat egg whites until foamy, add cream of tartar. Beat until soft peaks form, add vanilla and pureed banana little by little. Beat until stiff peaks form.

2 Spoon egg white into a greased 25cm (10in) pie plate. Shape with back of a spoon to form a shell.

3 Bake in a 110°C (225°F) oven for 1½ hours. Turn heat off, leave pie shell in oven for 2 hours with door half open.

4 Place milk in freezer, leave 2 hours.

5 Sprinkle peaches with almond essence and apricot liqueur. Leave to macerate for 2 hours.

6 Place cooled shell on a serving dish, fill with fruit. Whip chilled milk with a hand held electric mixer until stiff. Serve immediately.

Serves 8-10

Melon Rings with Berries

1 cantaloupe melon, chilled

½ punnet strawberries, chilled

½ punnet blueberries, chilled

1 Cut melon crosswise into 4 rings, 2.5cm (1in) thick. Remove seeds, do not remove rind.

2 Place rings on 4 dessert plates, cut inside rind to loosen flesh. Divide flesh into bite-size segments, leaving the shape of the ring intact inside the rind.

4 Arrange a mixture of strawberries and blueberries in the middle of each ring. Serve cold.

Serves 4

Pineapple with Walnut Raspberry Topping

4 pineapple rings, reserve juice

3 tblspn sugar

2 tblspn raspberry liqueur

¼ cup reserved pineapple juice

1 cup raspberries

½ cup walnut halves

1 Place a pineapple ring on each serving plate.

2 In a small saucepan combine sugar, raspberry liqueur and pineapple juice. Simmer gently for 8 minutes.

3 Add the raspberries and walnut halves, toss gently.

4 Spoon raspberry walnut topping over pineapple while warm and serve immediately.

Serves 4

Lemon Tequila Sorbet

1 cup water

1½ cups sugar

1 tblspn gelatine

1 tblspn hot water

⅓ cup freshly squeezed lemon juice

⅓ cup tequila

1 tblspn grated lemon rind

1 cup canned evaporated skim milk

1 Combine cup of water with sugar, boil 5 minutes.

2 Meanwhile dissolve gelatine in water. Add to syrup, stir until well combined.

3 Add lemon juice, tequila and lemon rind. Cool, combine with milk. Chill in refrigerator for 1 hour.

4 Place mixture in an ice-cream maker. Freeze according to manufacturer's instructions.

Serves 8

Pineapple with Walnut Raspberry Topping

Passionfruit Souffle with Raspberry Yoghurt Sauce

½ cup passionfruit pulp

2 tblspn lemon juice

¾ cup icing sugar

6 egg whites

RASPBERRY YOGHURT SAUCE:

125g (4oz) frozen raspberries

200g (6½oz) carton low fat plain yoghurt

1 tblspn sugar

1 tblspn Grand Marnier

1 Place passionfruit pulp, lemon juice and half the icing sugar in bowl, mix well. Beat egg whites until soft peaks form, add remaining sifted sugar gradually and continue beating until firm peaks form.

2 Gradually fold quarter of the egg whites into passionfruit mixture, then fold in remaining egg whites.

3 Lightly grease four individual souffle dishes (1 cup capacity). Sprinkle inside of each one with castor sugar, shake away excess. Spoon souffle mixture into dishes, bake in hot oven for 10 minutes or until risen and golden. Dust tops with sifted icing sugar immediately. Serve with Raspberry Yoghurt Sauce.

4 To make raspberry yoghurt sauce: Push raspberries through sieve to remove seeds. Combine raspberries with yoghurt, sugar and Grand Marnier.

Serves 4

Baked Strawberries and Almonds

2 tblspn slivered almonds

½ cup apricot jam

2 tblspn Grand Marnier

2 tspn sugar

2 punnets strawberries, hulled

1 Toast almonds on oven tray in moderate oven 5 minutes.

2 Warm jam, Grand Marnier and sugar in small saucepan.

3 Arrange strawberries in shallow ovenproof dish. Pour sieved jam mixture over strawberries.

4 Sprinkle almonds on top, bake in moderate oven 5 minutes or until heated through.

Serves 4

Baked Strawberries and Almonds

Apple and Raspberry Snow

3 Granny Smith apples, peeled, cored and sliced

2 tblspn castor sugar

2 tblspn water

125g (4oz) frozen raspberries, thawed

2 egg whites

⅓ cup castor sugar, extra

2 tblspn flaked almonds

1 Place apples in pan with sugar and water. Cover, cook gently, stirring occasionally, for 10 minutes or until apples are tender.

2 Blend or process with raspberries until smooth. Spread mixture in base of shallow ovenproof dish.

3 Beat egg whites until soft peaks form, gradually add extra sugar until mixture forms a meringue. Spread meringue over apple mixture. Smooth top, bake in moderate oven for 5 minutes or until golden.

4 Toast flaked almonds on oven tray in moderate oven for 5 minutes. Serve dessert sprinkled with toasted flaked almonds.

Serves 4

Pears in Champagne with Raspberries

2 large ripe pears

½ cup dry champagne

½ cup unsweetened pear juice (from can pears in own juice)

½ tspn vanilla essence

1 tspn arrowroot

2 tspn water

⅓ cup fresh raspberries

1 Peel, halve and core pears. Slice thinly leaving each half attached at stem end. Arrange sliced pears in shallow dish in a single layer.

Flambe Peaches

2 Combine the champagne, pear juice and vanilla in small pan, cook for 5 minutes. Add combined arrowroot and water, cook until mixture boils and thickens. Pour mixture over pears and stand for 2 hours.

3 Serve pear halves fanned onto individual dessert plates and pour champagne sauce over each. Garnish with raspberries.

Serves 4

Mango Mousse

2 mangoes, peeled and seeded

1 tblspn sugar

2 tblspn gelatine

¼ cup water

¾ cup evaporated skim milk

1 Blend or process mangoes until smooth. Combine sugar and mango puree in bowl.

2 Sprinkle gelatine over water, dissolve over hot water, add to mango mixture.

Mango Mousse

3 Beat milk in a bowl until frothy, fold into mango mixture. Pour into 4 serving dishes, refrigerate until set.

Serves 4

Flambe Peaches

8 ripe peaches, peeled

½ cup castor sugar

¾ cup water

⅓ cup Kirsch

1 Heat sugar and water in small pan until sugar is dissolved. Add peaches, simmer, covered, 5 minutes. Turn peaches once half way through cooking.

2 Add 1 tablespoon Kirsch, cook 3 minutes. Arrange peaches and syrup on serving plate.

3 Place remaining ¼ cup Kirsch in small pan, heat for 30 seconds, light with match and pour over peaches.

Serves 4

Stone Fruit Salad

4 ripe peaches, stoned

8 ripe apricots, stoned

4 ripe nectarine, stoned

1 mango

2 cups cherries, pitted

·1 tblspn chopped mint

1 Cut peaches, apricots and nectarines into wedges. Peel mango, cut into slices.

2 Combine fruit in bowl with cherries and mint. Chill before serving. Serve with sweetened low fat plain yoghurt if desired.

Serves 4

Strawberry and Orange Crepes

CREPE BATTER:

¼ cup plain flour

2 egg whites, beaten

½ cup skim milk

1 tspn oil

STRAWBERRY FILLING:

⅓ cup low fat cottage cheese

1 tblspn sugar

½ tspn grated orange rind

3 tspn orange juice

250g (½lb) punnet strawberries, sliced

STRAWBERRY SAUCE:

125g (4oz) strawberries

2 tspn orange juice

1 Sift flour into bowl, make well in centre, gradually stir in combined egg whites, milk and oil, mix to smooth batter, allow to stand for 15 minutes.

2 Heat a small frying pan, lightly brush with oil, add quarter of the batter to pan, cook until set and lightly browned underneath. Turn crepe carefully, cook other side. Repeat with remaining batter.

3 Divide filling between crepes, fold into quarters, serve with sauce.

4 To make strawberry filling: Combine sieved cottage cheese, sugar, rind and juice in bowl, mix well, stir in strawberries.

5 To make strawberry sauce: Blend or process strawberries and juice until smooth, strain.

Serves 4

Yoghurt Passionfruit Ice-Cream

2 tblspn honey

200g (6½oz) carton low fat plain yoghurt

1 tspn gelatine

2 tspn water

1 egg white

1 passionfruit

1 Combine honey and yoghurt in a bowl, mix well.

2 Sprinkle gelatine over water, dissolve over hot water, cool 2 minutes, stir into yoghurt mixture. Spread into sandwich tin, cover with foil, freeze 2 hours or until set.

3 Transfer yoghurt mixture to small bowl of electric mixer, beat until mixture thickens and doubles in bulk, transfer to a large bowl.

4 Beat egg white until firm peaks form, fold into yoghurt mixture with passionfruit. Pour back into sandwich tin, cover, freeze 3 hours or until set.

Serves 4

Yoghurt Passionfruit Ice-cream

INDEX

TEMPERATURE AND MEASUREMENT EQUIVALENTS

OVEN TEMPERATURES

	Fahrenheit	Celsius
Very slow	250°	120°
Slow	275–300°	140–150°
Moderately slow	325°	160°
Moderate	350°	180°
Moderately hot	375°	190°
Hot	400–450°	200–230°
Very hot	475–500°	250–260°

CUP AND SPOON MEASURES

Measures given in our recipes refer to the standard metric cup and spoon sets approved by the Standards Association of Australia.

A basic metric cup set consists of 1 cup, ½ cup, ⅓ cup and ¼ cup sizes.

The basic spoon set comprises 1 tablespoon, 1 teaspoon, ½ teaspoon and ¼ teaspoon. These sets are available at leading department, kitchen and hardware stores.

IMPERIAL/METRIC CONVERSION CHART

MASS (WEIGHT)
(Approximate conversions for cookery purposes.)

Imperial	Metric	Imperial	Metric
½ oz	15 g	10 oz	315 g
1 oz	30 g	11 oz	345 g
2 oz	60 g	12 oz (¾ lb)	375 g
3 oz	90 g	13 oz	410 g
4 oz (¼ lb)	125 g	14 oz	440 g
5 oz	155 g	15 oz	470 g
6 oz	185 g	16 oz (1 lb)	500 g (0.5 kg)
7 oz	220 g	24 oz (1½ lb)	750 g
8 oz (½ lb)	250 g	32 oz (2 lb)	1000 g (1 kg)
9 oz	280 g	3 lb	1500 g (1.5 kg)

METRIC CUP AND SPOON SIZES

Cup	Spoon
¼ cup = 60 ml	¼ teaspoon = 1.25 ml
⅓ cup = 80 ml	½ teaspoon = 2.5 ml
½ cup = 125 ml	1 teaspoon = 5 ml
1 cup = 250 ml	1 tablespoon = 20 ml

LIQUIDS

Imperial	Cup*	Metric
1 fl oz		30 ml
2 fl oz	¼ cup	60 ml
3 fl oz		100 ml
4 fl oz	½ cup	125 ml

LIQUIDS (cont'd)

Imperial	Cup*	Metric
5 fl oz (¼ pint)		150 ml
6 fl oz	¾ cup	200 ml
8 fl oz	1 cup	250 ml
10 fl oz (½ pint)	1¼ cups	300 ml
12 fl oz	1½ cups	375 ml
14 fl oz	1¾ cups	425 ml
15 fl oz		475 ml
16 fl oz	2 cups	500 ml
20 fl oz (1 pint)	2½ cups	600 ml

* Cup measures are the same in Imperial and Metric.

LENGTH

Inches	Centimetres	Inches	Centimetres
¼	0.5	7	18
½	1	8	20
¾	2	9	23
1	2.5	10	25
1½	4	12	30
2	5	14	35
2½	6	16	40
3	8	18	45
4	10	20	50
6	15		

NB: 1 cm = 10 mm.